MARK TWAIN

LITERATURE AND LIFE SERIES
(Formerly Modern Literature and World Dramatists)
GENERAL EDITOR: PHILIP WINSOR

Selected list of titles:

SHERWOOD ANDERSON *Welford Dunaway Taylor*
JAMES BALDWIN *Carolyn Wedin Sylvander*
SAUL BELLOW *Brigitte Scheer-Schäzler*
ANTHONY BURGESS *Samuel Coale*
TRUMAN CAPOTE *Helen S. Garson*
WILLA CATHER *Dorothy Tuck McFarland*
JOHN CHEEVER *Samuel Coale*
JOSEPH CONRAD *Martin Tucker*
JOAN DIDION *Katherine Usher Henderson*
JOHN DOS PASSOS *George J. Becker*
THEODORE DREISER *James Lundquist*
T. S. ELIOT *Burton Raffel*
WILLIAM FAULKNER *Joachim Seyppel*
F. SCOTT FITZGERALD *Rose Adrienne Gallo*
FORD MADOX FORD *Sondra J. Stang*
JOHN FOWLES *Barry N. Olshen*
ROBERT FROST *Elaine Barry*
ELLEN GLASGOW *Marcelle Thiébaux*
ROBERT GRAVES *Katherine Snipes*
ERNEST HEMINGWAY *Samuel Shaw*
CHESTER HIMES *James Lundquist*
JOHN IRVING *Gabriel Miller*
CHRISTOPHER ISHERWOOD *Claude J. Summers*
SARAH ORNE JEWETT *Josephine Donovan*
JAMES JOYCE *Armin Arnold*
KEN KESEY *Barry H. Leeds*
RING LARDNER *Elizabeth Evans*
D. H. LAWRENCE *George J. Becker*
C. S. LEWIS *Margaret Patterson Hannay*
SINCLAIR LEWIS *James Lundquist*
ROBERT LOWELL *Burton Raffel*
NORMAN MAILER *Philip H. Bufithis*
BERNARD MALAMUD *Sheldon J. Hershinow*
MARY MCCARTHY *Willene Schaefer Hardy*
CARSON MCCULLERS *Richard M. Cook*
JAMES A. MICHENER *George J. Becker*

(*continued on last page of book*)

MARK TWAIN

Robert Keith Miller

FREDERICK UNGAR PUBLISHING CO.
NEW YORK

Library of Congress Cataloging in Publication Data

Miller, Robert Keith, 1949–
  Mark Twain.

  (Literature and life series)
  Bibliography: p.
  Includes index.
  1. Twain, Mark, 1835–1910—Criticism and interpretation.
I. Title.   II. Series.
PS1338.M5 1983   818'.409   82-40269
ISBN 0-8044-2627-9 (cloth)
ISBN 0-8044-6496-0 (pbk.)

First paperback edition, 1984

For Steven and Delia Darvas

Contents

Chronology

November 30, 1835   Samuel Langhorne Clemens is born in Florida, Missouri, the fifth child of John Marshall and Jane Lampton Clemens.

Autumn 1839   John Marshall Clemens moves his family to Hannibal, Missouri (pop. 450).

March 24, 1847   John Clemens dies of pneumonia.

May 1, 1852   "The Dandy Frightening the Squatter" appears in *The Carpet Bag,* a weekly humor magazine published in Boston. This is the first published work by Samuel Clemens.

April 9, 1859   Samuel Clemens is licensed as a Mississippi River pilot.

Spring 1861   The outbreak of the Civil War leads Clemens to leave the Mississippi and join a battalion of Confederate irregulars.

July 18, 1861   Samuel Clemens leaves for Nevada with his brother Orion, who has been appointed secretary of the territory—a reward for campaigning on behalf of Lincoln.

Fall 1861–Summer 1862   Clemens tries to make his fortune prospecting for gold and silver.

August 1862   Clemens joins the Virginia City *Territorial Enterprise* as a full-time reporter and feature writer.

February 2, 1863   Clemens uses the name "Mark Twain" for the first time.

June 1864   Moving to San Francisco, Clemens joins the staff of the *Morning Call* and begins to write for the *Californian,* under the editorship of Bret Harte.

November 18, 1865   *The Saturday Press* in New York prints "The Celebrated Jumping Frog of Calaveras County." The story is widely reprinted, and Twain begins to acquire a national reputation.

March 7, 1866   Clemens sails for Honolulu, having contracted to write travel letters for the Sacramento *Union.*

October 2, 1866   Mark Twain makes his debut as a public speaker, offering a humorous lecture in San Francisco on his experiences in Hawaii.

December 15, 1866   Twain leaves for New York as correspondent for the *Alta California*. He arrives in the city January 12, 1867, after a difficult journey.

April 25, 1867   Charles Webb publishes Twain's first book, *The Celebrated Jumping Frog of Calaveras County, and Other Sketches*.

June 8, 1867   As a reporter for the *Alta California*, Twain sails for Europe aboard the *Quaker City*, a cruise ship taking a group of affluent Americans on a five-month tour of the Mediterranean.

November 21, 1867   Elisha Bliss, of the American Publishing Company in Hartford, Connecticut, proposes that Twain write a book based on his trip to Europe.

December 27, 1867   Twain meets Olivia Langdon, the sister of a fellow passenger on the *Quaker City*.

November 17, 1868   Twain begins his first American lecture tour with a speech in Cleveland on "The American Vandal Abroad."

July 1869   *The Innocents Abroad* is published by Elisha Bliss.

August 14, 1869   Twain becomes a part owner of the Buffalo *Express*, thanks to the generosity of Jervis Langdon, his future father-in-law.

November 1869   Twain lectures in Boston and meets William Dean Howells, who will be his friend and literary advisor for over forty years.

February 2, 1870   Samuel Clemens and Olivia Langdon are married in Elmira, New York.

July 1870   Twain contracts with Bliss to write a book about Nevada and California within six months.

August 6, 1870   Jervis Langdon dies of cancer, attended by both his daughter and son-in-law.

November 7, 1870   Olivia Clemens gives birth to a son. He is named Langdon.

Fall 1871   The Clemens family moves to Hartford, Connecticut.

February 1872 *Roughing It* is published by Elisha Bliss.

March 19, 1872 The Clemenses have a second child, a daughter whom they name Olivia Susan, but who will be known as Susy.

June 2, 1872 Langdon Clemens dies of diphtheria.

Winter 1873 Twain writes *The Gilded Age* in collaboration with his Hartford neighbor, Charles Dudley Warner.

December 1873 *The Gilded Age* is published by Elisha Bliss.

June 8, 1874 Clara Clemens, a second daughter, is born to Samuel and Olivia Clemens.

Summer 1874 At Quarry Farm, near Elmira, New York, Twain begins *Tom Sawyer* and adapts *The Gilded Age* for the stage.

September 1874 The Clemens family moves into their elaborate nineteen-room house at 351 Farmington Avenue, Hartford. On the 16th, *The Gilded Age* opens in New York, starring the celebrated comedian John T. Raymond as Col. Sellers. It is an immediate success, earning Twain an average of $900 a month well into the following winter.

January 1875 The first of seven installments of "Old Times on the Mississippi" appears in the *Atlantic Monthly*.

June 1876 "The Facts Concerning the Recent Carnival of Crime in Connecticut" is published in the *Atlantic*.

Summer 1876 Twain begins *Huckleberry Finn* at Quarry Farm.

October 1876 Twain collaborates with Bret Harte on a comedy, *Ah Sin*. It is finished by December, but their relationship is irreparably strained.

December 1876 *Tom Sawyer* is published by Elisha Bliss, over a year after he had received the manuscript and too late for the Christmas trade. Twain begins to think about changing publishers.

July 31, 1877 *Ah Sin* opens in New York at the Fifth Avenue Theatre. It closes after five weeks, losing money for the producers.

November 1877   Twain begins *The Prince and the Pauper*.

December 17, 1877   Twain makes his "Whittier Birthday Speech."

Spring 1878–Summer 1879   The Clemens family is in Europe, principally in Germany. Twain gathers material for *A Tramp Abroad*.

March 1880   *A Tramp Abroad* is published by Elisha Bliss.

July 26, 1880   Jean Clemens is born—Twain's fourth and last child.

April 1881   Twain appoints his nephew Charles L. Webster as his business manager.

December 1881   *The Prince and the Pauper* is published in Boston by James R. Osgood.

April 1882   Twain returns to the Mississippi to gather material for the second half of *Life on the Mississippi*. He will tour the Mississippi River valley until the end of May.

Summer 1883   Twain finishes *Huckleberry Finn* at Quarry Farm. *Life on the Mississippi* is published by James R. Osgood.

Winter 1884   In order to secure greater control over his books, Twain establishes the Charles L. Webster Publishing Co.

February 18, 1885   *The Adventures of Huckleberry Finn* is published by Charles L. Webster & Co.

March 1885   The Library Committee of Concord, Massachusetts, describes *Huckleberry Finn* as "trash and suitable only for the slums." It expels the book from its shelves, inaugurating a history of censorship that afflicts the work to this day. Nonetheless, *Huck* sells 51,000 copies by May.

December 1885   Charles L. Webster & Co. publishes *The Memoirs of Ulysses S. Grant*. The book earns over $400,000 for the Grant family, rescuing them from bankruptcy, and Twain becomes convinced that he has a genius for business.

January 1886   Twain begins *A Connecticut Yankee in King Arthur's Court*.

Fall 1886   Twain takes over half ownership of the Paige Typesetter, promising to underwrite all expenses for building, manufacturing, and promoting the machine.

December 1889   *A Connecticut Yankee in King Arthur's Court* is published by Charles L. Webster. Twain secures all rights to the Paige Typesetter in exchange for $160,000 plus the promise of $25,000 a year for seventeen years.

October 1890   Jane Clemens dies at the age of ninety.

Spring 1891   The Clemens family closes their house in Hartford and moves to Europe hoping to economize. They will live abroad for most of the next nine years.

April 16, 1894   *Tom Sawyer Abroad* is published by Charles L. Webster.

April 18, 1894   Mark Twain declares bankruptcy, ruined by his investments in the Paige Typesetter—still unmarketable fourteen years after Twain had first become involved with it. Henry H. Rogers of Standard Oil becomes his financial advisor, and he insures that all Twain's copyrights pass to Olivia Clemens as principal creditor.

November 1894   *Pudd'nhead Wilson* is published by the American Publishing Co.

July 1895   Twain begins a round-the-world lecture tour in order to pay his debts. During the next year, he will visit the Pacific Northwest, Australia, New Zealand, Ceylon, India, and South Africa.

May 1896   *Personal Recollections of Joan of Arc* is published by Harper & Brothers.

August 18, 1896   Alone in England, Twain learns that his daughter Susy has died of meningitis in Hartford.

November 1896   *Tom Sawyer, Detective* is published by Harper & Brothers.

November 1897   *Following the Equator* is published by the American Publishing Co.

January 1898   Twain pays off his debts in full.

October 15, 1900   Mark Twain returns to America.

February 1901   "To the Person Sitting in Darkness" is published in the *North American Review*.

June 5, 1904   Olivia Clemens dies of heart disease.

Fall 1904   Twain settles at 21 Fifth Avenue, his home for the next four years.

December 5, 1905   Harper & Brothers gives a gala dinner at Delmonico's to celebrate Twain's seventieth birthday. Guests as disparate as Willa Cather and Andrew Carnegie wish Twain well.

January 1906   Twain authorizes Albert Bigelow Paine to be his official biographer.

June 1907   Twain receives an honorary Doctorate of Literature from Oxford University. He is entertained at Windsor Castle by Edward VII.

June 1908   Twain moves into his last home—Stormfield, an Italianate villa in Redding, Connecticut.

October 1909   Clara Clemens marries the pianist Ossip Gabrilowitsch. She leaves with him for Europe, leaving her father alone with Jean.

December 24, 1909   Jean Clemens dies of an epileptic seizure while taking a bath.

Winter 1910   Twain's health begins to fail rapidly.

April 21, 1910   Mark Twain dies of angina pectoris.

1

vvvvvvvvvvvvvvvvvvvvvvvvvvvvvvvvvvvvvvvvvvvvvvv

The Lincoln of
Our Literature

Visiting Samuel Clemens in the luxurious home he had
recently built for himself in Hartford, Connecticut,
William Dean Howells asked his friend why it is that
men so often hate the past. And Clemens responded
with a simple explanation: "It's so damned humiliating."[1]

By the time Clemens made this remark, he had
achieved for himself an international reputation as
"Mark Twain," the most popular American writer of
the late nineteenth century. He was happily married to
the only woman he ever really loved, and he had
achieved what most men would regard as great wealth.

But in many respects, his life was a litany of regret. A Westerner in the East, he was extremely sensi-
tive to any sign that he was not accepted by the people
he affected to scorn. He never forgave a Boston ma-
tron who refused to have him at her dinner table. He
quarreled with Bret Harte for making fun of his furniture. And as late as 1907, when Oxford University
awarded him an honorary doctorate of letters, he felt a
great need for recognition, writing that it helped purge
him of "thirty-five years' accumulation of bile and injured pride."[2]

But Twain could never entirely overcome the
sense that his critics might be right. A favorable review
in the prestigious *Atlantic Monthly* meant so much to
him early in his career that he was moved to call upon

the editor in person in order to express his thanks. And when—at the height of his career—he made a very funny speech to an audience that was not prepared to be amused, he later wrote abject letters of apology to the principal guests, convinced that he was guilty of unforgivably bad taste. His persistent sense of inadequacy was apparent to those who knew him. One acquaintance went so far as to declare that "his whole life was one long apology."[3]

Personal idiosyncrasies aside, there were many events in Twain's life that any man would regret. His wife, and three of their four children, would all die before him. And he would go bankrupt when he was nearly sixty. The wonder then is not that Twain was "humiliated" by the past, but that he was able to rise above it, drawing upon his experience to create several of the most important works of American literature.

Samuel Langhorne Clemens was born on November 30, 1835, in the "almost invisible" village of Florida, Missouri—then the border of the American frontier. His father, John Marshall Clemens, had originally come from Virginia, where his family had been reasonably well to do, "gentlefolk but not magnates." They traced their ancestry back to Geoffrey Clement, one of the judges who sentenced Charles I to death, a genealogy that was never clearly established but afforded Twain much pleasure. And on his mother's side, Twain was encouraged to believe himself related to the rightful Earl of Durham.

Despite this distinguished lineage, John and Jane Clemens were far from affluent when their son Samuel was born, two months premature. He was their fifth child, and the family was crowded into a two-room shack. It seemed unlikely that the newborn infant would survive the winter. But the man we know as

Mark Twain would see out the first decade of the twentieth century. And death would take other children in the family instead: Margaret in 1839, Benjamin in 1842, and Henry in 1858.

Twain remembered his father as "a proud, a silent, austere man" who considered himself to be a member of the professional class both by virtue of his birth and by the fact that he had studied law. He was justice of the peace in Florida, and he owned three slaves, having inherited them upon the death of his own father. Moreover, he was the owner of a 75,000-acre estate in Tennessee—land that he had purchased for $500 shortly after his marriage, convinced that he was securing his family's eventual fortune.

But if he believed that his family would one day be rich, John Clemens nonetheless had to admit that their present status was precarious. Consequently, in 1839 he moved his family to Hannibal, Missouri, where he hoped to find prosperity commensurate with his sense of self-worth.

Destined to be immortalized as St. Petersburg, Hannibal seemed to be a town with a future. It was not much larger than Florida, but it was on the Mississippi, and steamboats called several times a day. John Clemens quickly became one of the town's principal citizens—president of the Hannibal Library Institute, and active in any plan for civic improvement. But he did not prosper. Instead, he lost most of his property by backing the note of a friend who went bankrupt. And in March 1847, he died of pneumonia, leaving behind a family of five. His son Samuel was eleven.

Samuel Clemens was a difficult child, given to mischief and misadventure. He barely escaped drowning on nine separate occasions, and he was often found sleepwalking. His father's death was a calamity for which he was not prepared. Albert Bigelow Paine,

Twain's official biographer, offers the following glimpse of the young Clemens, based on Twain's own dictation fifty-nine years after the event.

The boy Sam was fairly broken down. Remorse, which always dealt with him unsparingly, laid a heavy hand on him now. Wildness, disobedience, indifference to his father's wishes, all were remembered; a hundred things, in themselves trifling, became ghastly and heart-wringing in the knowledge that they could never be undone. Seeing his grief, his mother took him by the hand and led him into the room where his father lay.

"It's all right, Sammy," she said. "What's done is done, and it does not matter to him any more; but here by the side of him now I want you to promise me—"

He turned, his eyes streaming with tears, and flung himself into her arms.

"I will promise anything," he sobbed, "if you won't make me go to school! Anything!"

His mother held him for a moment, thinking, then she said: "No, Sammy; you need not go to school any more. Only promise to be a better boy. Promise not to break my heart."[4]

And as this suspiciously melodramatic vignette draws to a close, the grief-stricken boy promises to be trustworthy, brave, clean, and reverent. Victorian mothers were perfectly capable of making their children swear to be good over a suitably decorous corpse, and it is possible to see this as a pivotal moment in Twain's life. But allowance must be made for the distortions of memory, especially since "the properties of the open coffin and the dreadful oath suggest the imagination of Tom Sawyer," as Bernard DeVoto has observed.[5]

On the other hand, what we know of Jane Clemens makes it possible for us to see her acting out this faintly macabre scene. An extraordinarily good woman, who was remembered by her son as "the natural ally and friend of the friendless," she was not the sort of person who could be trifled with. Twain admired "her soldierly qualities," and he always remembered how on a trip to St. Louis she seized a whip from a man who was beating a horse and shamed him into promising to reform. And she had a similar effect upon a dissolute character in Hannibal who chased his daughter down the street one day, threatening to beat her with a heavy rope. Mrs. Clemens threw open her front door and gave the girl shelter. She then locked the door behind her and stood without flinching as the man threatened and abused her. In Twain's words: "She did not flinch or show any sign of fear; she only stood straight and fine and lashed him, shamed him, derided him, defied him in tones not audible to the middle of the street but audible to the man's conscience and dormant manhood."

Whatever its effect upon his son's character, the death of John Clemens forced additional economies upon his survivors. Within a year, Samuel Clemens was apprenticed to a local printer, Joseph P. Ament. He worked for nearly two years for Ament, leaving him in October 1850, in order to join the Hannibal *Western Union*, a small weekly newspaper that had recently been bought by Orion Clemens.

Twain's older brother Orion was to spend his life wandering from one business scheme to another, failing at every project to which he turned with enthusiastic incompetence. And he was almost always short of cash. He promised his brother a good wage but was seldom able to pay it. By 1853, Twain was ready to try to make his own way. In May of that year, at the age of seventeen, Samuel Clemens left Hannibal for St. Louis, New York, and Philadelphia. For the next two years, he supported himself—often only just barely— as a typesetter for a variety of newspapers and private firms, while enjoying what would prove to be the first of many travels. But by the spring of 1855, he was once again working for Orion, now a printer in Keokuk, Iowa.

By this time, Samuel Clemens had discovered the joy of seeing his words in print. He had contributed a variety of sketches to Orion's paper and as early as 1852 had published his first story in a national magazine. But he had no intention of becoming a writer; he wrote simply because he found it easy to write, and he still had no clear idea what he wanted to do with his life. He was bored by his work in Keokuk and eager to leave town when, in November 1856, he had a piece of extraordinary luck. While walking down the street, he happened upon a fifty-dollar bill—a great deal of money in pre-Civil War America. His mother's son, he advertised the money for four days, during which no one claimed it. At that point, he felt entitled to use it himself. He bought a ticket for Cincinnati, where he secured work and remained the rest of the winter.

During the winter he read a book about the Amazon, and he decided that his fortune would be assured if he could only get to Brazil. With this goal in mind, he left Cincinnati in April on board a New Orleans-bound steamboat piloted by Horace Bixby. The young Twain must have had charm, for he was able to persuade Bixby to let him help steer the boat—no trivial task on a river as treacherous as the Mississippi. Upon arriving in New Orleans, Twain abandoned his South American plans and convinced Bixby to make him his apprentice. Pilots, in those days when steamboating was at its height, made very good money, over $200 a month. Bixby agreed to teach Twain what he knew for $500, $100 in advance, and the new "cub pilot" was able to borrow that amount from his brother-in-law, William A. Moffet of St. Louis.

Twain's experiences in "learning the river" form the nucleus of *Life on the Mississippi*, which will be discussed in the next chapter. But one event of his eighteen-month apprenticeship is too important to pass over. In the spring of 1858, Twain was temporarily working for another pilot, a Mr. Brown, on board the *Pennsylvania*. He arranged a job on the boat for his younger brother Henry.[6] Brown seems to have been a tyrant, and he regularly abused both young men. Finally, he went too far, striking Henry in the face—and prompting Sam to knock him flat with a stool. Although he expected to be dismissed, Sam was simply transferred to another vessel when the boat reached port. On the night before the *Pennsylvania* was to leave for the return trip upriver, Henry was urged by his older brother to remember that it was his duty to help the passengers, in case of accident, and not simply look out for himself.

A few days later, the *Pennsylvania* exploded just south of Memphis. Henry was blown clear of the ship, but he was not injured. Instead of swimming to shore, he swam for what remained of the boat so that he could help survivors. As he approached the wreck, his lungs were penetrated by scalding steam. He was brought to a hospital in Memphis, and Sam found him there just in time to watch him die. Under the circumstances, it was hard for him not to blame himself for his brother's death.

Twain became a licensed pilot in April 1859, and he practiced this profession until the outbreak of the Civil War. Years later, Horace Bixby would declare: "Sam was never a good pilot. He knew the Mississippi River like a book, but he lacked confidence. . . . Being a coward, he was a failure as a pilot."[7] And while Mark Twain would make much of the romance of piloting, he was happy enough to leave it when the time came. But as DeLancey Ferguson has argued, Bixby's testimony may be inaccurate.[8] He was interviewed in 1908 about events that had occurred fifty years previously. It is unlikely that he would have agreed to work as a partner with Clemens in 1858, and again in 1860, if the young man were really a "coward." It is more probable that he was simply a safe and conscientious pilot, unwilling to take the bold risks we find Bixby taking in *Life on the Mississippi*.

The Mississippi was already being blockaded when Samuel Clemens made his last trip up the river, disembarking at St. Louis in April 1861. By June, he was back in Hannibal where he joined a battalion of Confederate "irregulars"—volunteers who did not formally enlist. He became a second lieutenant in the "Marion Rangers" and spent two weeks marching about in the rain, mostly in retreat from wherever Union soldiers had been reported. Many years later, Twain would describe this experience in "The Private History of a Campaign that Failed."

Early in the Lincoln administration, Orion Clemens had one of his few pieces of good luck. He had supported Lincoln in the bitter election of 1860 and was rewarded with an appointment as secretary to the territory of Nevada, an office that combined—according to his brother—"the duties and dignities of Treasurer, Comptroller, Secretary of State, and Acting Governor in the Governor's absence."[9] When he headed west to take office, he was accompanied by his younger brother, who was by now both out of work and anxious to avoid military service.

For the next three years, Samuel Clemens lived in Nevada. At first, he was convinced that he would make his fortune by mining for the gold and silver that then seemed to flow unchecked from the famous Comstock Lode. But he also began to contribute occasional pieces to the territory's leading newspaper, the Virginia City *Territorial Enterprise*. It is to Twain's credit that he realized he was a failure as a prospector, and in August 1862 he accepted an offer from the *Enterprise* to join its staff as a full-time reporter for twenty-five dollars a week, walking over sixty miles through uninhabited country in order to take up his post.

By virtue of both his personal charm and his position on the *Enterprise*, Clemens became an important figure in Virginia City, his company sought after and his opinion respected. It was at this time that he first began to call himself "Mark Twain."[10] And he also became acquainted with Artemus Ward, then America's leading western humorist and a master of the lecture platform. Studying Ward's manner, Twain began to learn the art that he would eventually perfect—the comic lecture made all the more amusing by a dry and apparently naive delivery.

As the result of an editorial he wrote about a rival newspaperman, Twain was challenged to a duel in the spring of 1864. The duel was never fought. But Nevada was on the brink of statehood, and the legislature had recently made dueling a felony in an attempt to make it seem as if the frontier days were over. Twain was advised to remove himself beyond the reach of territorial law, and so in June 1864, he moved to San Francisco where he joined the staff of the *Morning Call*.

Twain soon found his work on the *Morning Call* to be "killingly monotonous and wearisome." In his *Autobiography*, he described what his work on the *Call* was like:

After having been hard at work from nine or ten in the morning until eleven at night scraping material together, I took the pen and spread this muck out in words and phrases and made it cover as much acreage as I could. It was fearful drudgery, soulless drudgery, and almost destitute of interest.

Not surprisingly, his work began to suffer, and he was fired—for the first and only time in his life.

But it was while he was in San Francisco that Twain began to move beyond journalism. He contributed to the *Californian*, a respected literary magazine edited by Bret Harte. And in November 1865, he published a story in a New York paper that was to win him national attention: "The Celebrated Jumping Frog of Calaveras County." Widely reprinted, this story can be said to mark the real beginning of Twain's career as a writer.

Shortly after "The Jumping Frog" appeared, Twain made another important step in furthering his career. He contracted with the Sacramento *Union* to go to Hawaii, then called the Sandwich Islands, and write a series of letters about island life. Regular steamer service had recently been established between Honolulu and San Francisco, and there was considerable interest throughout California in the commercial possibilities of what would one day become the fiftieth state. Twain sailed in March 1866, and he remained in Hawaii until the following July.

The most memorable of Twain's experiences in the Islands occurred late in his tour. The *Hornet,* an American clipper ship, had gone down at sea, but after forty-three days in an open boat fifteen emaciated survivors reached Oahu. Although bedridden with saddle boils, Twain had himself carried on a stretcher to the hospital where the survivors were being treated. He wrote all night and got his story on board a ship leaving for San Francisco the next morning. His account was the first to reach the mainland, and it established his fame sufficiently for him to be invited to give a lecture on the Sandwich Islands upon his return to San Francisco. The advertisements for this lecture, which marked Twain's debut as a public speaker, concluded with a characteristically wry note: "Doors open at 7 o'clock. The trouble begins at 8 o'clock."

Held at Maguire's Academy of Music, the lecture was an enormous success. Twain subsequently went on to lecture throughout California and Nevada, but within two months he was ready for a new venture.

Twain's adventures in the West would eventually provide him with the material for *Roughing It*. But the experience of writing travel letters led directly to his successful career as a lecturer and, more importantly, it established the pattern for his first book, *The Innocents Abroad*. That work still lay almost two years ahead. But, on the strength of his letters from the Sandwich Islands, Twain was able to contract for a series of letters to be written from New York for another newspaper, the *Alta California*.

On December 15, 1866, Samuel Clemens left San Francisco for New York by the fastest means then available. He sailed down the Pacific Coast to Nicaragua, crossed overland by mule and wagon, and on reaching the Atlantic boarded a New York–bound ship. The journey proved to be hazardous. Cholera broke out on board ship, and nine passengers died. But the thirty-one-year-old author fortified himself with brandy and looked confidently ahead, his true vocation found at last.

The man who descended upon New York City in January 1867 must have seemed extraordinary, even by the standards of that jaded metropolis. He later claimed that, at this point in his life, he was so handsome that "even inanimate things stopped to look." Of medium height and delicate build, he had an unusually large head, luminous red hair, and "fine blue-greenish eyes" surmounted by brows that were "like a sort of plumage." [11] Combining the boldness of a frontier with the insouciance of a dandy, he affected an elaborately Western manner, accompanied it with an exaggerated Southern drawl, and dressed in a way that was calculated to draw attention to himself. He outraged one hostess by wearing an outfit of yellowish-brown pants with a gray jacket and a violet bow tie. This predilection for sartorial splendor would grow even more pronounced in the years ahead. When he became prosperous, Twain loved to parade about in a sealskin coat and hat. As an old man he would make a fetish out of white suits. And he wore his scarlet academic robe from Oxford to his daughter's wedding, delighted to have an excuse—however feeble—to show it off in public.

During his first months in New York, Twain enjoyed exploring the city's low life; on one occasion he was even arrested for brawling and forced to spend a night in jail. But if he had simply wanted to amuse himself, he might easily have stayed in San Francisco. Twain was ambitious, and he brought to New York a letter of introduction to Henry Ward Beecher, at that time the most famous minister in the country. Beecher had him to dinner in his home and introduced the budding writer to his sister Harriet Beecher Stowe, the commercially successful novelist who would one day be Twain's neighbor in Hartford. And it was through Beecher that Twain learned of a chance to go abroad.

Prominent members of Beecher's Brooklyn congregation were organizing a combination pilgrimage and pleasure trip. Nominally led by one of Beecher's Sunday school superintendents, the group would tour the Holy Land—but only after visiting the world's fair, then being held in Paris, and calling at the principal cities of Italy. An enthusiastic traveler and a writer eager for material, Twain was able to convince the *Alta California* to send him along on the trip. The expense was considerable: $1,250 for the boat, plus $500 in gold for land expenses. Twain's own fare was paid by his paper, but the trip would have been worth almost any price, for from it came *The Innocents Abroad*, the book that freed Twain from the grind of daily journalism.

The group's ship, the *Quaker City*, sailed from

New York in early June, a little less than six months
after Twain's arrival in the East. The passengers would
be together almost constantly for the next five months,
and several would never grow reconciled to the cigar-
smoking, whisky-drinking Twain. But he made a
number of friends, two of whom would play important roles in his subsequent life. Mary Fairbanks, the
matronly wife of a Cleveland publisher, was quickly
drawn to Twain. Early in the trip, she recorded that
"all eyes are turned toward Mark Twain. . . . Sitting
lazily at the table, scarcely genteel in his appearance,
there is something, I know not what, that interests and
attracts."[12] An intelligent and cultivated woman, she
was soon to become Twain's confidante and advisor,
helping to initiate him into the mysteries of polite respectability. Twain welcomed her advice and willingly submitted to her his correspondence so that she
could edit it for him, deleting anything improper. He
was even seen at one point tearing up an entire manuscript and throwing the pieces overboard, because Mrs.
Fairbanks had disapproved. He called her "Mother"
and would do so for the next thirty-two years. As Justin Kaplan has observed: "Mary Fairbanks was the
kind of civilizing influence that Huck Finn lit out from,
but which Clemens courted for years."[13]

    The civilizing influence of Mary Fairbanks would
be put to good use in the year immediately following
the cruise, as Twain began to court the twenty-two-
year-old sister of another passenger on the ship, Charles
Langdon. In the midst of a predominantly middle-
aged group, Twain was happy to have a friend who
was close to his own age. Their backgrounds differed
enormously; Langdon came from a rich family in up-
state New York that had been active Abolitionists. But
their intimacy grew, and late in the trip—while the
ship lay moored in the Bay of Smyrna—Langdon

showed his friend an ivory miniature of his sister Olivia. Twain liked to claim, in later years, that he fell in love with her at once.

When the *Quaker City* returned to New York in November 1867, Twain went straight to the offices of the New York *Herald,* where he wrote a humorous but harsh account of the trip that was published the next day. And the day after this article appeared, Elisha Bliss of the American Publishing Company wrote to Twain, proposing that he write a book about his experiences abroad.

Twain was slow to commit himself, however. He had already agreed to go to Washington as private secretary to Senator William M. Stewart of Nevada, while serving also as the Washington correspondent for Horace Greeley's New York *Tribune.* His income would be much reduced if he decided to write a book. It would mean, he realized, reducing his newspaper correspondence to one or two letters a week at a time when such letters seemed a sure guarantee of success. But Washington did not agree with Twain, and few men were less suited to work as a private secretary. By the end of February 1868, Samuel Clemens had decided to write the book that would make his name known across America.

Based in Hartford, Connecticut, the American Publishing Company was a subscription house; its books were sold door to door, primarily in communities that could not sustain a bookstore—or in neighborhoods where the inhabitants would never think of entering such a store, but who might be tempted into buying a volume or two through ingenious marketing. Salesmen would roam the countryside, carrying with them sample bindings, a sample chapter, and a pile of illustrations. Many customers were poorly educated, and since it was impossible to inspect the book itself, much emphasis was attached to the number of pages that were for sale. The subscription system therefore tended to force writers into writing long books—often longer than their contents justified. The book would be printed only when enough copies had been sold in advance to make the venture profitable for all three of the parties involved: the publisher, the author, and the canvasser.

This system made padding almost inevitable. And while profits could be considerable, many writers preferred to publish elsewhere. Subscription publishing was considered to be commercial—best suited for family Bibles and home medical advisors. It is a measure of Twain's accomplishment that, when *The Innocents Abroad* appeared, it was favorably reviewed in spite of the fact that it was a subscription book—the sort of label that tended to condemn a work in advance among those for whom literature was something elevated and refined.

Twain's contract called for a work of 240,000 words, and he completed this task by drawing heavily upon the correspondence he had written during the trip, editing it and reshaping the character of the narrator, but reprinting much that had already appeared in the *Alta California*. The owners of that paper believed, quite reasonably, that they had invested a lot of money in Twain's trip, and they wanted to publish a collected edition of the letters for their own benefit. Twain had to make a special trip to California to resecure the right to his material. Legally, these letters now belonged to the *Alta*, but Twain was persuasive, and he still had many influential friends in California; after a month's negotiations, he regained control over his correspondence, and the work went ahead.

A month after the *Quaker City* had returned to New York, Charles Langdon invited Twain to meet his family, who were then visiting the city in order to hear Charles Dickens give a public reading at Steinway

Hall. No one in the Langdon family seems to have seen that Twain took an unusual interest in their beautiful daughter—despite a thirteen-hour-long visit on New Year's Day 1868—and by the time the Langdons left for home, Twain had won an invitation to come and stay with them.

Jervis Langdon, the family patriarch, had made his fortune during the Civil War by controlling the coal and iron monopoly for the region surrounding Elmira and Buffalo, New York. The huge mansion that he built for his family in Elmira expressed not only his great wealth, but also an almost majestic commitment to Victorian values. And his daughter Olivia was a model Victorian heiress. Like Elizabeth Barrett Browning, she was a beautiful invalid. Partially paralyzed by a fall when she was sixteen, Livy—as she was called—spent two years bedridden in a darkened room, unable to move until she was commanded to do so by a mind healer.[14]

The Langdons were generous hosts, but when they received Samuel Clemens as a guest in their home, they saw him simply as a friend of their son's, not as a prospective son-in-law. Their guest was no longer simply a journalist, however; the impending publication of *The Innocents Abroad* had improved his social status. And Twain seems to have had a remarkable ability to get what he wanted. He wanted Olivia Langdon to be his wife, and by Thanksgiving 1868 they were engaged—although the Langdons kept the engagement secret until the following February, giving them time to investigate the strange man who had come to claim their daughter.

A surprising number of Twain's references proved to have nothing good to say about him. Letters came to Elmira describing him as "a humbug" and a man who "would fill a drunkard's grave," prompting Jervis Langdon to ask the embarrassed suitor, "What kind of

people are these? Haven't you got a friend in the
world?" Clemens responded, "Apparently not."[15] And
it is a tribute to Langdon's sagacity that he nonetheless
decided to welcome Twain into his family. It must
have been clear to him that his daughter was very
much in love, and as he would be dead of cancer in little over a year, he was probably also motivated by an
understandable desire to see her settled before he died.

Samuel Clemens married Olivia Langdon in February 1870, after a formal engagement of one year.
Their thirty-three-year marriage would be exception-
ally happy—something to which almost everyone who
knew them testified at length. Their letters suggest a
love affair that never grew cold, and despite radically
different backgrounds, they achieved a wonderful
sense of rapport.

In order to insure that his daughter would be well
provided for, Langdon purchased for Twain a one-
third share of the Buffalo *Express*. He also gave the
newly married couple a fully furnished mansion in a
fashionable part of Buffalo. Six months later, he was
dead. And his daughter, pregnant and exhausted from
nursing him, had a nervous collapse.

Throughout the grim summer of 1870, Twain was
hard at work at a new book; another subscription
book, it was to be about his experiences in the West.
Roughing It, as it came to be titled, was promised for
January 1, 1871, less than a year after Twain's marriage. And the strain of completing it amid the con-
sternation caused by the death of his father-in-law, the
death—in his house—of one of his wife's friends, his
wife's subsequent collapse, and the birth of his first
child—a son, Langdon—brought the writer close to
breaking down. In his *Autobiography*, Twain recalled
these months as "among the blackest, the gloomiest,
the most wretched of my long life."

Unable to complete *Roughing It* on time, Twain

decided to get away from Buffalo. He listed for sale
both his house and his share in the *Express,* and in the
spring of 1871 took Livy to her sister's summer home,
Quarry Farm, in the hills overlooking Elmira.[16] During
the next fifteen years, Quarry Farm would be important to Twain. He would bring his family there every
summer and do much of his best writing in a special
study that was designed for him and set apart from the
rest of the house. Both he and his wife would find at
the farm a retreat from increasingly demanding lives.

In the autumn of 1871, Twain moved his family to
Hartford, Connecticut, the city that would be their
home for the next twenty years. He rented the house of
John Hooker, the husband of Henry Ward Beecher's
sister Isabelle, and the direct descendant of the Thomas
Hooker who founded Connecticut in the mid-seven-
teenth century. Hooker owned a hundred-acre tract of
woodland on the western fringe of the city. Carefully
choosing his neighbors, he subdivided the land, realizing substantial profits, while creating around him an
unusual community of relatives and close friends who
shared an interest in art, literature, and politics.

The Clemens family quickly became an integral
part of this community. Known as Nook Farm, it included, in addition to the Hookers, Harriet Beecher
Stowe; Charles Dudley Warner, with whom Twain
would later write *The Gilded Age;* Francis Gillette, the
United States Senator from Connecticut; and his son
William, the distinguished actor. A few blocks away
lay the Asylum Hill Congregational Church, the minister of which—Joseph Twichell—became a particularly
close friend of Twain's. Hartford was then one of the
most prosperous cities in the East, the home not only
of Twain's publisher, but also the Remington and Colt
factories and several large insurance companies. New
York and Boston were easily accessible by train. And

Twain was happy to settle down at last, in what struck him as an ideal situation.

In 1874, Twain confirmed his residency in Hartford by building his own home, a nineteen-room architectural extravaganza that reflected both his originality and his status as a man of property.[17] Built of multicolored brick, it had the turrets of a castle and the promenades of a steamboat, five baths, a conservatory, and a separate coachhouse. A Hartford newspaper described the house as "one of the oddest looking buildings in the State ever designed for a dwelling,"[18] but Twain was proud of it and always eager to show it off. After spending over $100,000 on the house and its furnishings, he subsequently spent another $30,000 only a few years later, bringing Louis Tiffany in to redecorate and having landscapers reshape the lawn so that the house could be more easily visible from the street. He rejoiced in its notoriety, just as he rejoiced in his sealskin coat and white linen suits.

The years that Twain spent in Hartford were his most creative. These years would see the publication of most of his major works—from *Roughing It* in 1872 to *A Connecticut Yankee in King Arthur's Court* in 1889, shortly before deteriorating finances forced him to close his house and move his family to Europe in a futile attempt to economize. But bankruptcy was unimaginable in the early Hartford years, as Twain's reputation continued its rise, making the future seem infinitely promising. His personal happiness was marred only by the death of his eighteen-month-old son in June 1872, following an outing in which the absent-minded father had allowed a fur blanket that had been protecting the child to fall aside.

Despite his son's death, for which he always blamed himself, Twain enjoyed the resilience that springs from great expectations. At thirty-seven, he was still comparatively young. *Roughing It* was selling nearly as well as *The Innocents Abroad*. And the successful author had another child by now, upon whom his affection might be centered. His daughter Susy was born a few months before Langdon's death.

One indication of Twain's growing stature was the trip he took to England in August 1872. In London he was given a banquet by the Lord Mayor, praised by the Lord Chancellor, and urged to lecture by the man who managed Dickens. Although he had gone to England to gather material for a satirical book, that book would remain unwritten. For the moment at least, Twain was a confirmed Anglophile, and he returned to Britain the following spring, lecturing to capacity crowds on "Our Fellow Savages of the Sandwich Islands."

During the six months that separated these two English tours, Twain had thrown himself into completing another project, spending the winter of 1873 collaborating with Charles Dudley Warner on the novel that came to be called *The Gilded Age*. The two men agreed upon a basic plot—an exposé of corruption during the Ulysses S. Grant administration interwoven with a love story. Of the sixty-three chapters in the completed book, Twain claimed to have written thirty-five. The result cannot be ranked among Twain's major works, but it is not as chaotic as one might expect. The two authors subjected their material to criticism as they wrote, meeting each night to read aloud to their wives what they had written each day. The chief strength of *The Gilded Age* is the memorable characterization of Col. Mulberry Sellers, an American Micawber who is always broke but always optimistic.

Twain returned from his second English tour in January 1874, and the following spring and summer would be among the most fruitful in his life. In April the Clemens family returned to Quarry Farm, and a second daughter, Clara, was born to them there in June. And it was at this time that Twain began *The Adventures of Tom Sawyer,* the first of his books to deal with childhood and the Mississippi River valley in which he himself had grown up. He would not finish this book until the following summer, but his imaginative return to Hannibal may be responsible for the inspiration he had in October to write a series of articles for the *Atlantic Monthly* that would draw upon a related aspect of his youth. As Twain explained to William Dean Howells, then editor of the magazine, he had been talking to Joseph Twichell about "old Mississippi days of steamboating glory and grandeur as . . . [seen] *from the pilot house."* Twichell pointed out that this was "a virgin subject to hurl into a magazine," and Twain recognized its potential.[19] In the midst of moving into his new house in Hartford during the fall of 1874, Twain thus began to write about his years on the river. Collectively known as "Old Times on the Mississippi," the first of the essays that would be the genesis of *Life on the Mississippi* appeared in the January 1875 issue of the *Atlantic.* Others followed monthly through July, by which time Twain had returned to *Tom Sawyer* and completed it.

But, with the monthly installments of "Old Times on the Mississippi," the spring of 1875 brought with it th first signs that Twain's carefully structured world was beginning to disintegrate. Accused of committing adultery with one of his parishioners, Henry Ward Beecher was on trial in New York. And in Hartford, his two sisters were beginning to lose their wits. Deeply involved with spiritualists and clairvoyants, Isabelle Hooker had become convinced that she had a direct line to God. And in the house right next door to Twain's, Harriet Beecher Stowe—whose husband and son were both alcoholics—was already degenerating into a form of insanity in which her chief pleasure would eventually be to slip away from her nurse and, in Twain's words, sneak up "behind a person who was deep in dreams and musings and fetch a war whoop that would jump that person out of his clothes."[20]

Moreover, Twain was becoming increasingly ready to find fault with colleagues. His relations with Elisha Bliss were seriously strained when the publication of *Tom Sawyer* was delayed for more than a year after Twain had submitted the finished manuscript, thus helping to prepare the way for Twain's decision, some years later, to form his own publishing company. And Twain's relationship with Bret Harte, which had never been easy, began to sour when Harte came to stay in Hartford during December 1876 and the two men collaborated on a play that was based loosely on *Roughing It* and Harte's "The Heathen Chinee." Harte was a poor guest; he ridiculed practically everything about the Twain household and even seems to have mocked Livy. Twain would generously lend money to Harte for several more years, but he blamed Harte for the failure of their play, *Ah Sin,* and eventually denounced him publicly.[21]

Exactly a year after his ill-fated collaboration with Harte, Twain endured an embarrassment that amounted in his own eyes almost to disgrace. Asked to be one of the speakers at a public dinner honoring John Greenleaf Whittier on his seventieth birthday, Twain devised a comic tale about three western tramps who impersonate Emerson, Longfellow, and Holmes. His audience—which included Emerson, Longfellow, and Holmes—was not amused. William Dean Howells was "smitten with a desolating dismay" by the way in which Twain's address seemed to mock the reverence with which literary Boston held its patron saints.

There fell a silence, weighing many tons to the square inch, which deepened from moment to moment, and was broken only by the hysterical and blood-curdling laughter of a single

guest, whose name shall not be handed down to infamy.
Nobody knew whether to look at the speaker or down at his
plate. I chose my plate as the least affliction, and so I do not
know how Clemens looked, except when I stole a glance at
him, and saw him standing solitary amid his appalled and
appalling listeners, with his joke dead on his hands.[22]

Other accounts of the evening suggest that Howells
exaggerated Twain's predicament. But Twain was
convinced that he made a fool of himself before the
very people he most hoped to impress.

Four months later Twain took his family to Germany, where he would gather material for *A Tramp
Abroad.* He believed that his career was in decline. *Ah,
Sin* was an undeniable failure. Early sales of *Tom
Sawyer* were disappointing. And expenses were out-
pacing income. He did not realize that his greatest tri-
umphs were still before him: *A Connecticut Yankee in
King Arthur's Court, Pudd'nhead Wilson,* and, most
importantly, *The Adventures of Huckleberry Finn*—a
book that he had started the previous summer but
had been forced to shelve when his imagination failed
him. During the sixteen months he would stay in Europe, inspiration continued to elude him. Twain had to
force himself to write *A Tramp Abroad,* and he found
the work slow-going.

It was January 1880 before Twain was able to de-
liver the manuscript of *A Tramp Abroad,* but Bliss had
the book out within three months, as if to make
amends for his delay in printing *Tom Sawyer.* Twain
himself regarded the book as nothing more than a pot-
boiler, and given the way he had come to live, it was
requiring ever more money to keep his domestic fires
burning. Nonetheless, the book sold well—62,000 copies during its first year in print, his best sales since *The
Innocents Abroad.* But this was more indicative of the
almost insatiable demand for travel literature that accompanied the growth of wealth in late-nineteenth-

century America than a tribute to the quality of the
book per se. Another subscription book, *A Tramp
Abroad* is at least twice as long as it should be, padded,
among other things, with tall tales that bear a tangen-
tial relationship, at best, to the subject matter.

Cheered by the sales of his latest book, Twain
found his energy renewed. His last child, Jean, was
born in July 1880, as he completed *The Prince and the
Pauper* and reorganized his business affairs, abandon-
ing the American Publishing Company for James R.
Osgood of Boston. Twain's contract with Osgood was
unusual. According to its terms, Twain would finance
the production of his books and pay Osgood a $7\frac{1}{2}\%$
royalty for selling them, reversing the normal relationship between author and publisher and bringing
Twain a step closer to publishing his own books.

Osgood published *The Prince and the Pauper* in
December 1881, and the following April he accompanied Twain on the sentimental return to the Mississippi
River valley that is chronicled in the second half of
Life on the Mississippi. Victorian America took *The
Prince and the Pauper* to its heart; of all Twain's
books, it was one of the best-suited to please the official culture that then prevailed. But if there is nothing
in it to offend a nineteenth-century moralist, there is
almost nothing to interest the twentieth-century
reader. On the other hand, *Life on the Mississippi*—
published by Osgood in May 1883—is considered by
most critics to be the work that marked Twain's emergence as a great modern writer.

What's more, Twain's return to the Mississippi
seems to have hastened his rediscovery of the world he
had known as a child. Although he had worked sporadically at *Huckleberry Finn* since 1876, he was now
able to complete it, finishing the manuscript at Quarry
Farm during the summer of 1883. It had taken many
years to write, but Twain knew that here was a book of

which he could be proud. Writing to Andrew Chatto, his English publisher, he declared, "I've just finished a book, and modesty compels me to say it's a rattling good one, too."[23] Time has proved Twain's judgment sound. And as Justin Kaplan has observed, at this moment Twain reached "the high point of his creative life."[24]

Unfortunately, the years that were so creative for Twain as a writer were disastrous for him as a businessman. Like his brother Orion, Samuel Clemens had a fatal enthusiasm for schemes designed to make a fortune. Among other speculations, he invested $5,000 in a doubtful attempt to extract steam from coal, $32,000 in a new kind of steam pulley, and $41,000 in a printing process called Kaolotype. All of these ventures ended in financial loss and litigation. But Twain could have sustained these losses and continued to enjoy life on a grand scale were it not for two investments that came to dominate him.

In the winter of 1884, Twain established his nephew, Charles L. Webster, as a publisher. Webster had been acting as Twain's business manager since April 1881, and he impressed his uncle as shrewd and capable. In forming his own firm, Twain believed that he would secure greater control over his books, and it seemed at first as if he had made a wise move. Webster published *Huckleberry Finn* in February 1885. Despite the fact that it was condemned by the literary establishment—Louisa May Alcott, for example, primly declaring "If Mr. Clemens cannot think of something better to tell our pure-minded lads and lasses, he had best stop writing for them"[25]—the book sold 51,000 copies during its first three months in print, earning large profits.

And, in December of that year, Charles L. Webster Company brought off one of the great pub-

lishing coups of the nineteenth century when it offered, by subscription, *The Memoirs of Ulysses S.
Grant.* Despite the scandals that had marked his presi-
dency, Grant was still a national hero. His book reads
well, justifying the comparison Twain drew between it
and Caesar's *Commentaries.* But its phenomenal success can also be traced to the fact that Grant died of
cancer only a few months before his book appeared,
and the public was well aware that he had struggled to
complete his memoirs, even as he lay dying, so as to
save his family from bankruptcy. Presses had to be
kept running day and night in order to meet public
demand. And the book ultimately paid over $400,000
in royalties.

But both Twain and his nephew underestimated
the complexity of publishing, and nothing else they
published rivaled the deceptively easy success their
firm enjoyed during its infancy. Webster died in 1891,
burnt out at the age of forty, and Twain subsequently
blamed him for everything that went wrong with the
company that bore his name, even going so far as to
accuse him of addiction to drugs.[26] But Twain himself
must bear much of the responsibility for what followed. Charles L. Webster & Co. was his creation, and
while he interfered regularly in its affairs, he had too
many other interests to be able to give the concern the
close attention such an undertaking required. Moreover, he often asked Webster to do complicated er-
rands for him, leaving no one really in charge of day-to-
day operations. Undercapitalized and overextended,
Webster & Co. failed in 1894, taking with it $60,000 of
Twain's, $65,000 of Livy's, and leaving $97,000 in-
debtedness to other creditors—a debt which Twain
assumed.

Twain's publishing company failed in a year of financial panic; bankruptcies were common, and un-
employment ran high. But the firm might have been

able to weather a bad economy if Twain had not
linked its fate to another of his investments. For several years, he had been taking money out of the company in order to invest in a project that obsessed him:
the Paige Typesetter.

Twain expected this typesetter to revolutionize
the printing industry. In the hands of a skilled operator,
it could do the work of many printers, setting entire
words at a time and at a rate of up to twelve thousand
ems an hour—compared to only eight thousand ems an
hour on Linotype, the machine that ultimately captured the market. Designed by James W. Paige, it was
being built at the Colt arms factory in Hartford when
Twain made his first investment in it—for $5,000 in
1880.

On paper, the machine was a marvel. It had eighteen thousand separate parts and dazzled numerous in-
vestors at various demonstrations. Paige had obtained
his patent for it in 1874, ten years before the first Linotype was produced. But he was a perfectionist who
could never be satisfied. Whenever the machine
seemed about to be completed, its extraordinary in-
ventor would envision new improvements. With each
new improvement, the machine became more complex, and as it was constantly being taken apart and
redesigned, production costs continued to mount.
Constantly assuring Twain that the machine was almost finished—and that it required only one small ad-
justment—Paige charmed him into a fourteen-year
embroglio of increasingly serious financial significance.

Twain was so convinced that the machine would
make millions for him that in 1886 he made a major
commitment to it. Ignoring the advice of his business
advisor, he signed a contract with Paige in which he
promised to underwrite all the machine's expenses
from development through manufacture and promo-
tion in exchange for a half interest in it. Within a year,

this contract was costing Twain an average of $3,000 a month, and the more money the machine devoured, the more difficult it became to write the investment off. Three years after signing his first contract with Paige, Twain went on to sign another—guaranteeing the inventor $160,000 plus $25,000 a year for seventeen years in exchange for all rights to the machine. Nine years had by now passed since his first investment in the typesetter, but, urged on by Paige, Twain continued to pump money into it for another five years. It was 1894 before the machine got its first real test. It worked, but proved too delicate for regular commercial use. The mechanism was so complex that something or other was always breaking down. And by 1894, Twain was drained of resources. The failure that year of his publishing company found him with little to fall back upon, and he was forced into personal bankruptcy.

Twain could easily have disassociated himself from the Webster collapse, absorbing the loss he and his wife had sustained but acknowledging no personal liability for the rest of the firm's debts. His inclination seems to have been to take this course, and, given the state of the national economy that year, the creditors would probably have settled for partial repayment determined by the sale of the company assets. Olivia Clemens would not hear of this, however. She insisted that her husband pay back every penny that Webster & Co. owed, no matter what sacrifices had to be made. In this she had the surprising support of Henry H. Rogers, one of the founders of Standard Oil and a shrewd capitalist capable of great ruthlessness in business. He was a good friend to Twain, in his later years, and the beleaguered author frequently sought his advice. Rogers argued that a writer cannot indulge in the compromises that are customary among men of business; his income depends upon his popularity, and his popularity is likely to suffer if the public perceives him as weak in character.

Rogers represented Twain during the bankruptcy proceedings, and he promised the creditors that they would be paid in full if they would allow the author time to recoup. And through skillful negotiations, he managed to salvage some assets for the Clemens family. Since Webster owed Livy $65,000, Rogers insisted that she be considered a preferred creditor and that Twain's copyrights be turned over to her in exchange for this debt. And he also made sure that the Hartford house remained in the family—it was in Livy's name, and Rogers successfully argued that it was her personal property, upon which the creditors could make no claim.

Holding on to the copyrights made it possible for the family to recover. Twain himself had already tried to sell them to three leading publishers, none of whom were interested, believing that the books had already exhausted their market. But Rogers knew their potential worth, and he eventually negotiated a contract with Harper & Brothers that guaranteed Twain a minimum of $25,000 a year for the right to publish his collected works.

This contract was not signed until October 1902, however, and by that time Twain had already fought his way from beneath what had seemed an insurmountable pile of debt. In July 1895 he embarked upon a lecture tour that took him around the world. Accompanied by Livy and Clara, he lectured across Canada and then went on to Australia, New Zealand, Ceylon, India, and South Africa. The trip was a great success, and Twain forwarded all of the proceeds to Rogers, who invested the money wisely. His experiences are chronicled in his final travel book, *Following the Equator*. Published in

November 1897, it quickly sold 30,000 copies, and by
January 1898 Twain had paid his debts in full—a little
less than four years after declaring bankruptcy.

Perceived as a man of honor in an age in which
shoddy business practices were commonplace, Twain
was much respected for the way in which he had ful-
filled his obligations. When he returned to the United
States in the fall of 1900, after an unbroken absence of
over five years, he was proclaimed a hero by journal-
ists who found him to be consistently good copy. Until
his death ten years later, he would live to the accom-
paniment of public applause, a celebrity recognized
by millions who had not even read his books.

But just as Twain was beginning his financial recovery, he received a blow from which he never entirely recovered. At the conclusion of his around-the-
world lecture tour, he expected to reunite his family in
England, where he had rented a house for the summer
of 1896. Twain, Livy, and Clara reached England on
July 31. A week later, a letter arrived from Jean explaining that Susy was too ill to travel. The anxious
parents cabled for details and were assured that Susy's
recovery would be slow but certain. Livy and Clara
immediately sailed for America. But believing that the
danger had past, Twain remained in England in order
to work on his book.

Three days later, while Livy and Clara were in the
middle of the Atlantic, the unsuspecting father received a cable from Hartford, informing him that his
favorite daughter had died of meningitis. Twain was
devastated. He later reflected that "It is one of the
mysteries of our nature that a man, all unprepared, can
receive a thunder-stroke like that and live."

More misfortune was in store. When the diminished family returned to America, they rented a house
in Manhattan, just off Fifth Avenue. Livy was exhausted by the strain of housekeeping and attending to

innumerable social obligations, and by early 1902 she seemed headed for a nervous breakdown. Twain took her to Maine, believing that she might recover in the country, but her health continued to decline, and it was eventually necessary to hire a special train to bring the invalid back to New York. During the following winter, she was kept isolated from her husband, their communication limited to notes—and a five-minute visit in February, on the occasion of their thirty-third anniversary.

The exact nature of Livy's disease remains unclear. She was unquestionably old and frail, and she had a weak heart. But during her last years, she may also have suffered from the sort of nervous prostration that afflicted her when she was a girl. In any case, she was judged well enough to travel to Italy in the fall of 1903. It was hoped that the soft Italian climate would be better for her, but once they reached Florence, she remained bedridden and dependent upon cylinders of oxygen. On June 5, 1904, she finally died, leaving her husband plunged in grief and the daughters who had nursed her worn out. Jean suffered an epileptic seizure and spent many of the years that remained to her in various sanatoriums. And Clara had a breakdown that left her hospitalized for a year, forbidden by her physician to have any contact with her temperamental father.

Although enshrined after his death as a beneficent patriarch, Twain could not have been an easy man to live with. He could be wonderfully gentle and good-natured, but he could also break out into sudden flashes of temper. One Sunday morning, for example, he went through his drawers and threw out the window any shirt that had a missing button. Behavior such as this made relations with his children uncertain, and he once wrote to Howells that he had discovered that "all their lives my children have been afraid of me!"[27]

And Howells, who knew him well, later characterized Twain as capable of being "ruthlessly and implacably resentful," a man who, once crossed, could not forgive his enemies even when they were dead, feeling that "their death seemed to deepen their crimes."[28]

This was, of course, only a side of Twain, but it makes it easier for us to understand why Livy kept herself apart from her husband as she lay dying, and why Clara and Jean also moved away from him. Clara married a pianist and settled in Europe. And Jean, as we have seen, spent much of her adult life in sanatoriums and rest homes.

Of all the Clemens children, it was Jean who had the most difficult relations with her father. Like him, she seems to have been headstrong, and for several years father and daughter were almost estranged. During the last few months of her life, however, she grew close to Twain, moving with him to his last home— Stormfield, an Italianate villa in Redding, Connecticut—where she acted as his housekeeper and secretary. When Clara married in October 1909, Twain felt it "hard but I could bear it, for I had Jean left. I said *we* would be a family." But, two months later, Jean was dead—the victim of an epileptic seizure as she took a bath on Christmas Eve.

The day she died, Twain wrote "my life is a bitterness." His wife and three of their four children had all died before him, and the most famous writer in America now found himself alone in a "vast emptiness." He envied the dead, but would not envy long; having borne so much, he was asked to bear no more. Weakened by angina pectoris, the seventy-four-year-old "Lincoln of our literature"[29] was dead himself within four months, welcoming the release that came to him at sunset on April 21, 1910.

2

⁊⁊

Sailing a Shoreless Sea:
Life on the Mississippi

First published in 1883, *Life on the Mississippi* provides an ideal vehicle for commencing the study of
Twain's work. Within its pages are to be found almost
all aspects of that work as a whole. We find Twain as
novelist, autobiographer, and reporter offering up to
us a strange combination of memoir, travelogue, tall
tale, and literary manifesto, a potpourri into which in-
digestible hunks of raw statistics are haphazardly
thrown in beside some of the most evocative passages
in American literature.

The work originated in a series of articles Twain
wrote for the *Atlantic Monthly* in 1875 under the title
"Old Times on the Mississippi." They describe life
aboard the great paddle-wheel steamboats that made
their way up and down the river in the decade before
the Civil War; in particular, they focus upon the art of
piloting these ships through treacherous currents and
constantly shifting sandbars. This was a subject that
Twain knew well; moreover, it was both original and
well-suited to popular taste. The rapid industrializa-
tion of late-nineteenth-century America brought with
it one of the first of many waves of nostalgia for a
simpler past that continue to characterize American
culture. The articles proved to be successful, and it
was clear that there was a market for more material of
this sort.

Unfortunately, the articles in themselves were insufficient to make up a book, and Twain was uncertain how to expand them. Finally, he decided to return to the Mississippi, hoping that a river journey—his first in twenty years—would provide him with the new material he required. Accompanied by his publisher and a stenographer, Twain sailed from St. Louis to New Orleans, where he was received as an honored guest. He then traveled upriver all the way to St. Paul, Minnesota, much of the trip being completed on a boat captained by Horace Bixby, the man who had once taught the art of piloting to the young Sam Clemens.

Life on the Mississippi can thus be divided into two parts: the river remembered and the river reencountered. The first part is dominated by the material that had already been published in the *Atlantic;* the second, which can be said to begin at chapter twenty-two, tells the story of Twain's return to the river as a successful writer who is recognized and feted wherever he goes. As a result, the book lacks a unified point of view. The narrator shifts from pilot to tourist, and the river seen from a first class cabin is no longer the same as the river Twain remembered from his youth.

That Twain found it difficult to finish the book is evident from the text. Its organization is undeniably loose, and the author is frequently obliged to concede as much, admitting at one point, "But I am wandering from what I was intending to do," and confessing elsewhere that he has included an extraneous tale only because it is "a good story, not because it belongs here—for it doesn't." Moreover, Twain filled up many pages by quoting other travel writers to the extent of some eleven thousand words. When he finally finished the manuscript, he wrote to his business manager that he never wanted anything more to do with "this wretched God-damned book."[1]

But despite its shortcomings, *Life on the Mississippi* marks Twain's emergence as a great modern writer. Contemporary readers are apt to be struck by the way this work foreshadows *Huckleberry Finn*, and it has become something of a critical commonplace to see it as the raw material for his literary masterpiece. There is some truth to this, but the work deserves to be taken seriously in its own right and not simply in terms of its relation to *Huckleberry Finn*. For it was *Life on the Mississippi* that established Twain as something more than a western humorist; upon its publication it was quickly recognized as a "most solid book," in the words of an early reviewer, "more novel in its character, and even more American" than anything else Twain had yet written.[2]

Also, it may be that the divisions within the book have been overemphasized. Although there can be no question that the work would be stronger had it received more careful editing, there is certainly no reason to dismiss the entire second half as "dull and labored."[3] A careful reading of *Life on the Mississippi* will reveal that it is not as disorganized as it may seem. Despite numerous digressions, Twain seldom lost sight of several basic themes that provide an underlying unity to his apparently casual reminiscences.

The most obvious of these concerns is suggested by the book's structure, which contrasts the present with the past. Twain frequently seems to be an apostle of progress, delighting in the effect twenty years have had upon the Mississippi Valley. He is impressed by St. Louis, with its "solid expanse of bricks and mortar stretching away on every hand," and he claims that "the finest thing we saw on our Mississippi trip" was the sight that greeted him at New Orleans—"the white glare of five miles of electric lights." Relishing "a go-

ahead atmosphere which tastes good in the nostrils,"
Twain predicts even brighter days ahead: "The signs
are that the next twenty years will bring about some
noteworthy changes in the Valley, in the direction of
increased population and wealth and in the intellectual
advancement and the liberalizing of opinion which go
naturally with these."

Much has been made of this tendency of Twain's
"to celebrate the burgeoning industrial America he
saw all around him."[4] But it should be recognized that
Twain was very often ironic about the values he seems
to exalt. After he tours a sugar plantation, he reports:
"The cane is cultivated after a modern and intricate
scientific fashion too elaborate and complex to attempt to describe; but it lost $40,000 last year"—an
observation that suggests Twain's attitude toward tech-
nological innovation was not altogether uncritical. And
he seems very much aware that "progress" is a mixed
blessing: "We found a railway intruding at Chester, Illinois; Chester has also a penitentiary now, and is otherwise marching on."

The association we find here between penitentia-
ries and civic growth is characteristic. Twain's view of
history is cynical to say the least. Consider his account
of America's westward expansion:

How solemn and beautiful is the thought that the earliest pioneer of civilization, the van-leader of civilization, is never
the steamboat, never the Sabbath school, never the missionary—but always whisky! Such is the case. Look history over;
you will see. The missionary comes after the whisky—I
mean he arrives after the whisky has arrived; next comes the
poor immigrant with ax and hoe and rifle; next the trader;
next the miscellaneous rush; next the gambler, the desperado,
the highwayman, and all their kindred in sin of both sexes; and
next, the smart chap who has bought up an old grant that
covers all the land; this brings the lawyer tribe; the vigilance
committee brings the undertaker. All these interests bring

the newspaper; the newspaper starts up politics and a railroad; all hands turn to and build a church and a jail—and behold, civilization is established forever in the land. But
whisky, you see, was the van-leader in this beneficent work.
It always is.

This is a distinctly sour concept of "civilization." We
move from whisky to missionaries and on to poor im-
migrants, gamblers, desperados and highwaymen—
none of whom are attractive, and all of whom are destined to be replaced by only marginally more
respectable types, the speculators and lawyers, for
whom civilization is defined by party politics and funeral homes.

   And at least two important scenes are devoted to
ridiculing modern men of business. An oleomargarine
salesman from Cincinnati boasts that his product is so
cheap that "the whole country has *got* to take it," happily predicting the unappetizing prospect that we will
"see the day, pretty soon, when you can't find an
ounce of butter to bless yourself with." His spiel
prompts another salesman to brag about how his firm
puts false labels on cottonseed oil and sells it as im-
ported olive oil. "Maybe you'll butter everybody's
bread," he declares, "but we'll cottonseed his salad for
him from the Gulf to Canada, and that's a dead certain
thing." These men may be unfortunate examples of the
"go-ahead" types Twain praises elsewhere, but whether
or not they are representative of the American businessman in general, they are certainly singled out for
our scorn. Twain's own appraisal is succinct: "Brisk
men, energetic of movement and speech; the dollar
their god, how to get it their religion."

   Shortly afterward we get to meet a marvelously
self-confident undertaker who proclaims his trade "the
dead surest business in Christendom, and the nobbi-
est." Conversation with this gentleman reveals that he
is expert at tricking the poor into buying unnecessarily

expensive caskets. We learn that undertaking is extremely profitable: "There ain't anything equal to it but trading rats for di'monds in time of famine." Struck by the man's cheerfulness, the narrator asks, "If you are so lighthearted and jolly in ordinary times, what *must* you be like in an epidemic?" Explaining that bodies are buried too quickly during an epidemic to allow for embalming, our ever-efficient mortician remarks, "We don't like to see an epidemic. An epidemic don't pay."

Finally, Twain recognizes that industrial expansion is antithetical to natural beauty. In this respect, one passage in particular is worth quoting at length. Twain has been steaming through Iowa, and he records:

The majestic bluffs that overlook the river, along through this region, charm one with the grace and variety of their forms and the soft beauty of their adornment. The steep verdant slope, whose base is at the water's edge, is topped by a lofty rampart of broken, turreted rocks, which are exquisitely rich and mellow in color—mainly dark browns and dull greens but splashed with other tints. And then you have the shining river, winding here and there and yonder, its sweep interrupted at intervals by clusters of wooded islands threaded by silver channels; and you have glimpses of distant villages, asleep upon capes; and of stealthy rafts slipping along in the shade of the forest walls; and of white steamers vanishing around remote points. And it is all as tranquil and reposeful as dreamland, and has nothing this-worldly about it—nothing to hang a fret or a worry upon.

Until the unholy train comes tearing along—which it presently does, ripping the sacred solitude to rags and tatters with its devil's war whoop and the roar and thunder of its rushing wheels—and straightway you are back in this world, and with one of its frets ready to hand for your entertainment: for you remember that this is the very road whose stock always goes down after you buy it, and always goes up again as soon as you sell it.

It could easily be argued that Twain has presented us

with an unrealistically mellow view of nature—a nature that lacks both tooth and claw. It is a "dreamland," in which distant villages sleep and white steamers vanish around remote points. Words like "charm," "grace," "soft," and "tranquil," dominate the passage, and the diction as a whole suggests that Twain is romanticizing.

Be this as it may, it is evident that Twain sees nature as offering a welcome respite from the anxieties of modern life. There is nothing threatening about nature—"nothing to hang a fret or a worry upon." The "unholy train" is unwelcome because it shatters the "sacred solitude" that postindustrial man can enjoy only at rare intervals. The "roar and thunder of its rushing wheels" remind us that we are "back in this world," a world of noise, speed, and responsibility. Although there is an element of humor to the "fret" that springs most immediately to Twain's mind, we are nonetheless left with a clear contrast between pastoral tranquility and modern turmoil.

Because Twain perceives the unattractive side of "progress," he often seems to lament the past, conveying the sense that it was more picturesque, somehow, than the present. Having returned to the river after an absence of twenty years, he is shocked by the way in which things have changed. Consider, for example, the contrast that is drawn between two types of river men. Early in the book, Twain describes the men who guided barges down the river in his youth as

rough and hardy men; rude, uneducated, brave, suffering terrific hardships with sailorlike stoicism; heavy drinkers, coarse frolickers in moral sties . . . heavy fighters, reckless fellows, every one, elephantinely jolly, foul-witted, profane; prodigal of their money, bankrupt at the end of the trip, fond of barbaric finery, prodigious braggarts; yet, in the main, honest, trustworthy, faithful to promises and duty, and often picturesquely magnanimous.

Despite the catalog of negatives—"rough," "rude," "uneducated," "reckless," and "profane"—these men seem almost heroic. Everything they do is on a grand scale, be it lying, drinking, or fighting. Common sense suggests that there must have been some men, in those days, who were lazy, timid, or just plain mean. But we are dealing here with the archetypical, the American pioneer as sanctified by the warm glow of memory.

When Twain returns to the river, he is disappointed to find modern crews are apt to be less colorful:

Up in this region we met massed acres of lumber rafts coming down — but not floating leisurely along, in the old-fashioned way, manned with joyous and reckless crews of fiddling, song-singing, whisky-drinking, break-down-dancing rapscallions; no, the whole thing was shoved swiftly along by a powerful stern-wheeler, modern fashion, and the small crews were quiet, orderly men of sedate business aspect, with not the least suggestion of romance about them anywhere.

Similarly, although he recognizes that the Mississippi has been improved by the federal government, which has dredged out shallow channels and installed electric lamps at difficult crossings since he last traveled the river, Twain complains that life used to be more interesting. The river is now more easily navigable, but this has "knocked the romance out of piloting," and deprived pilots of the status they used to enjoy:

Verily we are being treated like a parcel of mates and engineers. The Government has taken away the romance of our calling; the Company has taken away its state and dignity.

In Twain's view, his old profession has now become a thing "of the dead and pathetic past."

The ultimate symbol of this vanished past is the steamboat itself. Twain recalls how such boats must have impressed the average passenger in the days when a river journey meant drama and adventure:

When he stepped aboard a big fine steamboat, he entered a
new and marvelous world: chimneytops cut to counterfeit a
spraying crown of plumes—and maybe painted red; pilot-
house, hurricane deck, boiler-deck guards, all garnished with
white wooden filagree work of fanciful patterns; gilt acorns
topping the derricks; gilt deer horns over the big bell; gaudy
symbolic picture on the paddle box, possibly; big roomy
boiler deck, painted blue, and furnished with Windsor arm-
chairs; inside, a far receding snow-white "cabin"; porcelain
knob and oil picture on every stateroom door; curving patterns of filagree-work touched up with gilding, stretching
overhead all down the converging vista; big chandeliers
every little way, each an April shower of glittering glass
drops; lovely rainbow light falling everywhere from the
colored glazing of the skylights; the whole a long-drawn, re-
splendent tunnel, a bewildering and soul-satisfying spectacle!

Twain himself seems to have stepped into "a new and
marvelous world." His description of the steamboat is
extraordinarily evocative, and the big white Mississippi steamer remains fixed to this day as a romantic
symbol of the American past, destined to be featured
prominently in endless snapshots from Disneyland,
where a pallid reproduction—bearing Twain's name—
ferries marveling suburbanites from one ersatz world
to another. Embarrassed by his own enthusiasm,
Twain subsequently tries to be more objective, pointing out that the towels were thin, and the decoration
sometimes "pretentious," but his vision of the steamboat remains, as a whole, both personal and affection-
ate, his prose as elaborate as the filagree-work he
delights to recall.

But, upon returning to the Mississippi, Twain is
forced to recognize that the great days of the steamboat are over. He is amazed by the sight of the St.
Louis wharves:

Half a dozen sound-asleep steamboats where I used to see a
solid mile of wide-awake ones. This was melancholy, this was

woeful. . . . Half a dozen lifeless steamboats, a mile of empty
wharves, a Negro fatigued with whisky stretched asleep, in a
wide and soundless vacancy, where the serried hosts of commerce used to contend! Here was desolation, indeed.

The steamboat has been superseded by the railroad—
just, as in our own day, the railroad would be out-
moded by the automobile. And the few boats that remain in use upon the river offer a sorry contrast to the
boats that Twain remembers. The first boat upon
which Twain attempts to book passage is appallingly
dirty:

She was a venerable rack-heap, and a fraud to boot; for she
was playing herself for personal property, whereas the good
honest dirt was so thickly caked all over her that she was
righteously taxable as real estate. There are places in New
England where her hurricane deck would be worth a
hundred and fifty dollars an acre.

Twain subsequently finds a more attractive boat, and
he is later impressed to find crew members wearing
uniforms. But he is nevertheless forced to conclude
that "as contrasted with what it was in its prime vigor,
Mississippi steamboating may be called dead."

Thus when Twain enthusiastically reports the
number of schools built in the various towns he visits,
the quantity of ice now manufactured in New Orleans,
and the tonnage of flour annually milled in St. Paul, he
should not be seen as a candidate for the Junior
Chamber of Commerce mindlessly extolling an uninterrupted flow of municipal wonders. Such passages
are more easily understood if we see them as a means
through which a hard-pressed writer sought to fill out
his text. A careful reading of *Life on the Mississippi* reveals that, so far from celebrating the "development"
of the Mississippi River valley, Twain was actually in-
clined to regret the passing of a world that, whatever

its shortcomings, seemed infinitely preferable to the world that had come to take its place.

What makes this elegy to the past surprising is that it occurs in a work that makes a sustained attack upon nineteenth-century romanticism. Twain laments the loss of romance on the Mississippi while simultaneously ridiculing romance as both dangerous and fraudulent—a fundamental conflict in values that makes *Life on the Mississippi* often seem at odds with itself.

Within this context, it would be useful to consider Twain's famous attack upon Sir Walter Scott. Blaming the Scottish novelist for checking the advancement of "liberty, humanity, and progress" that had come with the French Revolution, Twain sees Scott as a symbol of everything he had come to dislike about the American South:

Then comes Sir Walter Scott with his enchantments, and by his single might checks this wave of progress, and even turns it back; sets the world in love with dreams and phantoms; with decayed and swinish forms of religion; with decayed and degraded systems of government; with the silliness and emptiness, sham grandeurs, sham gauds, and sham chivalries of a brainless and worthless long-vanished society. He did measureless harm; more real and lasting harm, perhaps, than any other individual that ever wrote. Most of the world has now outlived . . . these harms, though by no means all of them; but in our South they flourish pretty forcefully still. There the genuine and wholesome civilization of the nineteenth century is curiously commingled with the Walter Scott Middle Age sham civilization and so you have . . . the duel, the inflated speech, and the jejune romanticism of an absurd past that is dead, and out of charity ought to be buried. But for the Sir Walter Scott disease . . . the South would be fully a generation further advanced than it is. It was Sir Walter Scott who made every gentleman in the South a Major or a Colonel, or a General or a Judge, before the war; and it was he, also, who made these gentlemen value their bogus decorations. For it was he that created rank and caste down there, and also reverence for rank and caste, and pride and pleasure in them.

Although Twain found that the South was changing, he was troubled by the number of "romantic juvenilities" that still survived. Dismayed by the Gothic Revival state capitol building in Baton Rouge, he observes:

Sir Walter Scott is probably responsible for the Capitol building; for it is not conceivable that this little sham castle would have been built if he had not run the people mad . . . with his medieval romances.

Similarly, Twain mocks a southern college for boasting in its prospectus that its architecture resembles "the old castles of song and story, with its towers, turreted walls and ivy-mantled porches." Such a school must be a "breeder and sustainer of maudlin Middle-Age romanticism." And when he finds another school praising its faculty for being southern by birth, rearing, and education, on the grounds that the South enjoys "the highest type of civilization this continent has seen," Twain responds by citing several stories taken from southern newspapers—stories that show generals and professors dying in senseless duels.

There is, of course, something arbitrary and capricious about Twain's attack upon Scott. It is difficult to believe that *Ivanhoe* helped start the Civil War—provocative though Twain's thesis may be. Moreover, we have seen how Twain himself tended to romanticize the past, the steamboat being to Twain what the castle was to Scott: a symbol of a picturesque way of life now past.

The virulence of Twain's attack upon Scott may well spring from the fact that he himself was something of a frustrated romantic. He tells us, for example, that as a cub pilot he never expected to have to leave a warm bed in order to help guide the boat: "I began to fear that piloting was not quite so romantic as I had imagined it was; there was something very real and worklike about this new phase of it." And as his education on the river continues, he learns that romance is the product of illusion, there seldom being anything romantic about that which is known and understood.

We see this most clearly in the account Twain provides of two ways of looking at the river:

Now when I had mastered the language of this water and had come to know every trifling feature that bordered the great river as familiarly as I knew the letters of the alphabet, I had made a valuable acquisition. But I had lost something, too. I had lost something which could never be restored to me while I lived. All the grace, the beauty, the poetry had gone out of the majestic river! I still keep in mind a certain wonderful sunset which I witnessed when steamboating was new to me. A broad expanse of the river was turned to blood; in the middle distance the red hue brightened into gold, through which a solitary log came floating, black and conspicuous; in one place a long, slanting mark lay sparkling upon the water; in another the surface was broken by boiling, tumbling wings, that were as many-tinted as an opal; where the ruddy flush was faintest, was a smooth spot that was covered with graceful circles and radiating lines, ever so delicately traced; the shore on our left was densely wooded, and the somber shadow that fell from this forest was broken in one place by a long, ruffled trail that shone like silver . . . and over the whole scene, far and near, the dissolving lights drifted steadily, enriching it, every passing moment, with new marvels of coloring.

Twain describes himself as having been "bewitched" by the river, and the passage in question here suggests that he was fully alive to its beauty. Unfortunately, "the romance and the beauty were all gone" once he learned to pilot the river. He is then forced to see the sun set through different eyes:

This sun means that we are going to have wind tomorrow; that floating log means that the river is rising . . . that slanting mark on the water refers to a bluff reef which is going to kill somebody's steamboat one of these nights . . . those tumbling "boils" show a dissolving sandbar and a changing channel there; the lines and circles in the slick water over yonder are a warning that that troublesome place is shoaling up dangerously; that silver streak in the shadow is the "break" from a new snag, and he has located himself in the very best place he could have found to fish for steamboats. . . .

Twain draws these observations to a close with an interesting analogy:

Since those days, I have pitied doctors from my heart. What does the lovely flush in a beauty's cheek mean to a doctor but a "break" that ripples above some deadly disease? Are not all her visible charms sown thick with what are to him the signs and symbols of hidden decay? Does he ever see her beauty at all, or doesn't he simply view her professionally, and comment upon her unwholesome condition all to himself? And doesn't he sometimes wonder whether he has gained most or lost most by learning his trade?

It is impossible to overlook the melancholy that permeates these reflections. What is less obvious is the way Twain has substituted one form of romance for another. There is absolutely no reason to assume, as he does, that every young woman with a rosy complexion is necessarily suffering from consumption. And who but a romantic would imply that knowledge is always disheartening? Innocence and experience may well be irreconcilable, but to claim that experience necessarily entails a loss is to fall victim to precisely the sort of ro-

manticism Twain claims to reject. And when we recognize the way in which he has turned the river and
the men who sail her into something larger than life, it
would be fair to say that, at this stage of his career,
Twain has an essentially romantic sensibility with
which he is ill at ease. Throughout *Life on the Mississippi,* he adopts a self-consciously modern voice—attacking sentimentality, demanding that writers abandon
the "flowery and idiotic" style characteristic of much
nineteenth-century prose, and admiring telegraphs
and electric lights whenever he possibly can. But at the
same time, we hear the persistent echo of another
voice, a quieter voice that speaks eloquently of the
vanished past—the preindustrial world.

The dissonance between these two voices tends to
confuse many readers. And on an immediate level
Twain's ambivalence toward romance is certainly responsible for what appear to be obvious contradictions within the book. Nonetheless, Twain's overt
attack upon romanticism provides the key to the underlying pattern of this work, revealing more extensive
thematic unity than is commonly perceived.

Despite his own predilection for the romantic,
Twain had come to see romance as an illusion—a type
of literary and aesthetic fraud. And, if we see *Life on
the Mississippi* as an attack upon dishonesty of any
sort, then several seemingly extraneous episodes
emerge to serve a similar purpose.

Early in the book we meet a night watchman who
entertains the young Twain with "a narrative that was
so reeking with bloodshed and so crammed with hair-
breadth escapes and the most engaging and unconscious personal villainies, that I sat speechless, enjoying,
shuddering, wondering, worshiping." The aspiring
cub pilot later discovers this man to be "a low, vulgar,
ignorant, sentimental, half-witted humbug, an untrav-

eled native of the wilds of Illinois." Twain does not
enjoy being disillusioned; he describes the experience
as "a sore blight." Later he tells us of his "chiefest
hero," a carpenter he knew as a boy: "He was a
mighty liar, but I did not know that; I believed everything he said. He was a romantic, sentimental, melodramatic fraud, and his bearing impressed me with
awe." One of the carpenter's boasts is subsequently
exposed, leaving him a "cheap and pitiful ruin" in
Twain's eyes: "He was a hero to me no longer but only
a poor, foolish, exposed humbug. I was ashamed of
him, and ashamed of myself." The last line is especially revealing; Twain sees himself as disgraced for
having been taken in. And it is extraordinary that he
should take such trivial incidents so seriously.

Almost as if in revenge for having been easily de-
ceived when he was young, Twain peoples *Life on the
Mississippi* with a steady procession of con-men. The
margarine and "olive oil" salesmen already discussed
fall within this category—as does the undertaker and a
pilot named Stephen who borrows large sums of
money that he has no intention of repaying. Such
scoundrels as these are partially redeemed by their
comic presentation, but they are kin to Murel and
Crenshaw, two utterly humorless villains who entice
slaves to "run away," promising to share with them the
reward money for their "capture" so that the blacks
can eventually buy their freedom. Later, they kill the
unsuspecting slaves in order to keep them from ever
bearing witness to the fraud.

Several of the tall tales that are woven into the
narrative also serve to illustrate Twain's fascination
with deceit. In one such story a seemingly innocent
farmer named John Backus is eventually revealed to
be a card shark who pretends to be a naif only so that
he can lure gamblers into playing for high stakes. And
a comparable hoax provides the plot for another tale,

in which a letter describes how a convict led a fellow prisoner to Christ. The letter is widely circulated and read at large assemblies, where it regularly reduces the pious to tears. Twain delights in proving the letter to be "a pure swindle," designed to inspire agitation for the release of the prisoner to whom it was supposedly addressed.

Even "A Dying Man's Confession," a tale set in Bavaria that seems completely inappropriate to a work chronicling life on the Mississippi, can be seen as providing another example of a swindle. The tale itself is a melodramatic account of murder, mistaken identity, and eventual retribution. It is neither moving nor amusing, but it prepares the way for an interesting scene. In the conclusion of the "confession," Twain ostensibly learns where ten thousand dollars is hidden—hidden, as it happens, in a small Arkansas town that the steamboat is approaching just as Twain finishes recounting what he had been told in Germany. He tells his traveling companions that he has undertaken the responsibility of finding the money and presenting it to a poor shoemaker, in accordance with the last wish of the man who had, on his deathbed, revealed the money's whereabouts.

Twain and his friends then begin to convince themselves that they have a moral responsibility to keep the money for themselves, arguing that so much money would probably corrupt the poor man for whom it was intended—he might "shut up his shop, maybe take to drinking, maltreat his motherless children," and "drift into other evil courses." Within moments they hypocritically decide that "Every sentiment of honor, every sentiment of charity, every sentiment of high and sacred benevolence warns us, beseeches us, commands us to leave him undisturbed. That is real friendship, that is true friendship." And once having come to this conclusion, it isn't long before the men begin to quarrel about how the money should be divided among themselves. This debate proves to be academic: we learn that the town in which the money was hidden is now entirely under water, having been washed away into the Mississippi. But as we watch the narrator and his respectable companions prepare to defraud someone of a substantial inheritance, we cannot help but feel that—given the right circumstances—almost anyone could become a cheat.

Seen within this context, Twain's attack upon Sir Walter Scott no longer seems self-indulgently digressive. Scott is simply the ultimate con-man, more dangerous than a card shark or an undertaker because he was able to deceive millions through literary sleight of hand, leaving behind him an infatuation with all that is false.

Even Twain's random comments on architecture and interior decoration can now be seen as thematically connected to the attack upon dishonesty that we find, in one form or another, in chapter after chapter. Twain's contempt for the Louisiana state capitol building is balanced by his praise for the Cotton Exchange in New Orleans; we are told that it has "no shams or false pretenses" about it. And when Twain satirically pictures a typical antebellum mansion, he emphasizes that it was designed to deceive. Its "imposing fluted columns and Corinthian capitals," for example, "were a pathetic sham, being made of white pine, and painted." And the fruit in the parlor proves to be "all done in plaster, rudely, or in wax, and painted to resemble the originals—which they don't."

But, while Twain sallies forth to do battle with all manner of frauds, he always comes back to the river, repeatedly stressing that the river, like the men who live along its banks, must be watched. Indeed, the

Mississippi may be the greatest imposter of all. It frequently changes its course, and it can mislead even a trained eye. Moreover, its beauty—as we have seen—is based upon illusion. It is almost as if Twain found in the Mississippi not only his subject, but also a perfect metaphor for the treachery he believed to be so pervasive. It is, in his words, "the crookedest river in the world." And as such it gave Twain the chance to explore all kinds of tricks and misconceptions.

If Twain seems obsessed with exposing lies, it is not because he was benevolently trying to protect his readers from lapsing into folly. Perhaps the most modern aspect of *Life on the Mississippi* is the way in which its author feels apart—almost to the point of alienation—from the world in which he finds himself.

Writing almost invariably demands at least some detachment from experience, but Twain often sounds detached to the point of cruelty. He is, for example, startlingly unsympathetic in his description of poor whites whose farms have been flooded:

Behind other islands we found wretched little farms, and wretcheder little log cabins; there were crazy rail fences sticking a foot or two above the water, with one or two jeans-clad, chills-racked, yellow-faced male miserables roosting on the top-rail, elbows on knees, jaws in hands, grinding tobacco and discharging the result at floating chips through crevices left by lost teeth; while the rest of the family and the few farm animals were huddled together in an empty wood flat riding at her moorings close at hand. In this flatboat the family would have to cook and eat and sleep for a lesser or greater number of days (or possibly weeks), until the river should fall two or three feet and let them get back to their log cabin and their chills again—chills being a merciful provision of an all-wise Providence to enable them to take exercise without exertion.

As Henry Nash Smith has observed, "To say that the men were 'roosting' on the fences degrades them to the level of animals."[5] And there is nothing amusing about Twain's claim that disease can be diverting.

Nor is this an isolated passage. Recalling an evening when his steamboat almost ran over a raft, Twain facetiously complains that "they happened to be fiddling . . . and we just caught the sound of the music in time to sheer off, doing no serious damage, unfortunately, but coming so near it that we had good hopes for a moment." After a lantern is brought, "the precious family stood in the light of it—both sexes and various ages—and cursed everything blue." In reporting this incident, Twain is almost certainly trying to be funny. But in describing the family in question as "precious," he adopts a tone that is distinctly unpleasant.

It should be recognized, however, that passages such as these occur primarily in the early chapters of the book, chapters that were written in a Hartford, Connecticut, study. Removed by both time and geography from his material, Twain may not have felt that poor whites were "real" so much as conveniently picturesque. When he returns to the river in the second part of the book, Twain continues to reveal a pronounced interest in the underside of life, but he is no longer so apt to treat it contemptuously.

Grim scenes abound, but as the work develops they become more realistic and consequently more distressing, for Twain as well as for his readers. Reliving a steamboat explosion, he tells us how a dying man "would tear off handfuls of the cotton and expose his cooked flesh to view," adding, "It was horrible." Later, we learn how a shell burst during the seige of Vicksburg cut a man's arm off "an left if dangling in my hand."[6] And when Twain attends a cockfight in New Orleans, he is horrified by the sight of the birds, "blind, red with blood," and groping about "with dragging wings." He is forced to leave:

I did not see the end of the battle. I forced myself to endure it as long as I could, but it was too pitiful a sight.

It is significant that only Twain is bothered by the proceedings:

I never saw people enjoy anything more than this gathering enjoyed the fight. . . . They lost themselves in frenzies of delight.

Thus, even when his sympathies are engaged by the actuality of suffering, Twain still stands alone and apart, isolated by the fact that others do not share his response.

Twain's return to Hannibal prompts him to recall an even more unsettling scene. And once again he is forced to turn away from death. A jail is burning with a tramp inside:

When I reached the ground, two hundred men, women, and children stood massed together, transfixed with horror, and staring at the grated windows of the jail. Behind the iron bars, and tugging frantically at them, and screaming for help, stood the tramp; he seemed a black object set against the sun, so white and intense was the light at his back. [The] marshal could not be found, and he had the only key. A battering ram was quickly improvised, and the thunder of its blows upon the door had been so encouraging a sound that the spectators broke into wild cheering, and believed the merciful battle won. . . . It was said that the man's death grip still held fast to the bars after he was dead; and in this position the fires wrapped around him and consumed him. As to this, I do not know. What was seen after I recognized the face that was pleading through the bars was seen by others, not by me.

This episode is based upon an incident Twain not only witnessed as a boy, but for which he felt responsible. It was he who had provided the tramp with the matches that had started the fire. He admits that he "saw that face, so situated, every night for a long time," and that "the impressions of that time are burned into my memory." But ultimately he disassociates himself from what had happened, claiming that remembering these events "entertains me as much now as they themselves distressed me then."

The visit to Hannibal that inspired this particular memory seems to have heightened Twain's sense of dislocation. Confronted with a town that differs from his memory of it, he is unable to believe what he sees:

I stepped ashore with the feeling of one who returns out of a dead-and-gone generation. I had a sort of realizing sense of what the Bastille prisoners must have felt when they used to come out and look upon Paris after years of captivity, and note how curiously the familiar and the strange were mixed together before them. I saw the new houses—saw them plainly enough—but they did not affect the older picture in my mind, for through their solid bricks and mortar I saw the vanished houses, which had formerly stood there, with perfect distinctness.

The comparison he draws between himself and prisoners leaving the Bastille is worth considering. From what, we must ask ourselves, does Twain see himself escaping? The past seems to have more meaning for him than the present—a present in which he is ill at ease and from which he is anxious to withdraw.

The vision of Hannibal that Twain prefers to keep before him is, on an immediate level, both charming and serene:

After all these years I can picture that old time to myself now, just as it was then: the white town drowsing in the sunshine of a summer's morning; the streets empty, or pretty nearly so; one or two clerks sitting in front of the Water Street stores, with their splint-bottomed chairs tilted back against the wall, pigs loafing along the sidewalk . . . two or three lonely little freight piles scattered about the "levee" . . . and the fragrant town drunk asleep in the shadow of them; two or three wood flats at the head of the wharf, but nobody to listen to the majestic, the magnificent Mississippi, rolling its mile-wide tide along . . . a sort of sea, and withal a very still and brilliant and lonely one.

But there are a number of disturbing elements within this seemingly idyllic description. There is nothing especially attractive about the drunk asleep in the shade or the pigs scattered about on the sidewalk. And the apparent serenity of the town is almost frightening. The streets are empty. Everyone is asleep. And as this "white town" drowses in the sun, even the great Mississippi is perceived to be "lonely"—like the freight piled on the levee. This is a vision of death rather than sleep. Isolated by the emptiness that stretches out all around him, it is Twain who feels "lonely," not the freight.

This sense of loneliness afflicts Twain throughout the book, but it is most remarkable in the material devoted to piloting. Although the historical record suggests otherwise, Twain claims to have loved his days as a pilot on the Mississippi. In an often quoted passage he explains,

If I have seemed to love my subject, it is no surprising thing, for I loved the profession far better than any I have followed since, and I took a measureless pride in it. The reason was plain: a pilot, in those days, was the only unfettered and entirely independent human being that lived on earth.

On the other hand, many years after the publication of *Life on the Mississippi,* he confessed,

There is never a month passes . . . that I do not dream of being in reduced circumstances, and obliged to go back to the river to earn a living. It is never a pleasant dream, either. I love to think about those days; but there's always something sickening about the thought that I have been obliged to go back to them.

And a careful reading of the text reveals what bothered Twain about piloting the river. The pilot may be "entirely independent" in the sense that he has complete control over the steamboat, but he is always mindful that the safety of its passengers and crew depends upon his skill. This then is the rub—he is independent of others, but others are not independent of him. The result is constant anxiety:

You find yourself away out in the midst of a vague dim sea that is shoreless, that fades out and loses itself in the murky distances; for you cannot discern the thin rib of embankment, and you are always imagining you see a straggling tree when you don't. The plantations themselves are transformed by the smoke, and look like a part of the sea. All through your watch you are tortured with the exquisite misery of uncertainty.

The situation portrayed here is almost Kafkaesque— the pilot lost upon a shoreless sea but nonetheless forced to move ahead, he knows not where.

It is hardly surprising to find Twain subsequently observing that his position as a pilot brought with it a "haunting sense of loneliness, isolation, and remoteness." He tries to convince us that "the tranquility is profound and infinitely satisfying," since the pilot is able to stand apart from "the worry and bustle of the world." But this is hard to believe. It is true that the pilot works within a self-contained world, remote from outside concerns, and this frees him, to an extent, from many of the anxieties that afflict men along the shore. His mind is entirely occupied by his work. But the responsibility this work entails is so great that the pilot always suffers from what Twain so beautifully calls "the exquisite misery of uncertainty."

Craving "independence" but fearing "loneliness," Twain was simultaneously attracted to and repulsed by the world of the steamboat pilot, just as he was both drawn to and repelled by the provincial society of his youth. In writing *Life on the Mississippi*, he was able to examine these basic conflicts, and with them his ambivalence toward "progress" and "romance." None of these conflicts find an easy resolution within its pages. But it is precisely this lack of certainty that makes the work so interesting to the modern reader. And in the years that lay ahead, Twain would continue to struggle with the dilemmas outlined in this, his first great work.

3

A Hymn Turned into Prose:
*The Adventures of
Tom Sawyer*

To enter the world of *Tom Sawyer* is to step into a world in which barefoot boys go fishing on mid-summer days, while prepubescent girls plan picnics on middle-class lawns and adults look beneficently on—dispensing ice cream, and advice that need not be taken seriously. The book offers to us a dream vision of American childhood. To be an American is to live on the edge of the frontier—but safely, behind a white picket fence in a town where everyone knows his neighbors and the sun beams down "like a benediction." And to be a child is to have adventures flavored with just enough anxiety to be genuinely exciting before returning, at will, to well-laden dinner tables and Sunday school socials. Rightly recognized as "the most amiable of all Mark Twain's novels,"[1] *The Adventures of Tom Sawyer* has been so thoroughly absorbed into the mainstream of American culture that "such incidents as the whitewashing of the fence are, like a familiar landscape, so intimate to our experience that their importance is easily forgotten."[2]

But a careful reading of *Tom Sawyer* reveals that childhood is not free of threats nor small towns free of fear. For all of its Norman Rockwell sort of charm, St.

Petersburg, Missouri, is not as idyllic as it may seem at first glance. The Temperance Tavern serves liquor in a back room. The graveyard is in poor repair. And there are caves, nearby, in which one can easily be lost. Moreover, as Bernard DeVoto observed many years ago, the episodes at the core of the book "revolve around body-snatching, murder, robbery, and revenge."[3] In short, St. Petersburg may be the garden of American innocence, but it is a garden in which a serpent lurks.

As the title of the book reminds us, we are concerned here not so much with a carefully structured narrative as with a series of "adventures" that are bound together by virtue of the fact that they are the adventures of one particular boy. These adventures occasionally overlap, but they are, for the most part, independent of one another, making the action of the novel so episodic that an impatient critic may go so far as to declare "there is no plot."[4] There are, however, four loose story lines that help hold the work together.

The first of these stories begins when Tom witnesses the murder of Dr. Robinson. Tom had gone to the graveyard at midnight, together with his good friend Huckleberry Finn, in order to act out a ritual that is supposed to cure warts. Hiding behind a tombstone, they see that Robinson has engaged two grave robbers to supply him with a corpse, presumably for the study of anatomy. The boys recognize the robbers as Injun Joe, a half-breed, and Muff Potter, the town drunk. A quarrel breaks out over money, and Robinson knocks Potter unconscious just before he himself is stabbed by Injun Joe. The murderer thereupon puts the bloody knife into Potter's hand, convincing him—when he comes to—that he killed the doctor in a drunken fit.

The boys, of course, know otherwise, and when Potter is imprisoned for the murder, Tom undergoes a crisis of conscience. He is afraid to tell the truth, believing that Injun Joe might easily kill him too. But he cannot bear to see Potter executed for a crime he did not commit. Summoning all his courage, Tom eventually brings himself to testify at Potter's trial. His dramatic evidence secures the man's release, but Injun Joe escapes from town before he can be arrested.

Although Tom relishes the celebrity that comes to him as the star witness at a murder trial, "Injun Joe infested all his dreams," making his nights "seasons of horror." He finds distraction, however, in courting Becky Thatcher, the dimpled daughter of the local judge. The growing relationship between Tom and Becky provides the material for another "adventure." During an outing to the labyrinthine caves outside of town, Tom leads Becky away from their classmates, and exploring further than the others dare to go, they finally realize they are lost. They are trapped within the caves for three days, and desperate search parties are almost ready to give them up when Tom discovers an opening to the surface.

By this point in the novel, Tom has won Becky's heart. But earlier in the story, they quarrel after Becky learns that Tom had once been "engaged" to Amy Lawrence. Seeing himself as "forsaken," Tom decides to run away from home. Together with Huck Finn and Joe Harper, he heads for Jackson's Island in the middle of the Mississippi. The boys play at being pirates and have a glorious time roasting turtle eggs and learning how to smoke. But the townspeople come to believe that the boys must have drowned in the river, and in a scene that represents the fulfillment of many a child's fantasy, Tom sneaks ashore to watch his family mourn his death. He subsequently returns to the island, but only to wait for his own funeral, which he and his friends enjoy unseen before revealing themselves to the astonished congregation. The boys are welcomed back from the dead, and Tom and Becky are soon reconciled.

A fourth and final story concerns the fate of Injun Joe. He returns to town to take revenge not on Tom but on the Widow Douglas, whose husband had treated him harshly. He plans to "slit her nostrils" and "notch her ears like a sow"[5] but is overheard by Huck who runs for help, scaring the culprit away. Seeking refuge in the same caves that proved so dangerous to Tom and Becky, he is accidently trapped inside when Judge Thatcher has the entrance triple-locked with a "big door sheathed with boiler iron," in order to prevent anyone else from becoming lost within. Several weeks elapse before his plight becomes known. "When the cave door was unlocked, a sorrowful sight presented itself in the dim twilight of the place. Injun Joe lay stretched upon the ground, dead, with his face close to the crack of the door, as if his longing eyes had been fixed, to the latest moment, upon the light and the cheer of the free world outside."

The villain conveniently disposed of, the novel now draws to a close with Tom and Huck falling joint heir to a little over twelve thousand dollars in gold— buried treasure that had been unearthed by Injun Joe and hidden by him in the cave, where the boys find it. As a result of this discovery, Huck is drawn into the social organization of the town, his share of the fortune invested at six percent, and his welfare entrusted to the Widow Douglas, who promises to raise the boy who had saved her from injury. And great things are predicted for Tom. Judge Thatcher declares that he is "no commonplace boy" and in gratitude for leading Becky out of the cave, promises to send him to West Point and later to "the best law school in the country."

As the various threads of the narrative unfold, they sometimes seem at odds with one another. Tom comes from a home where apples are carefully rationed, but when he leaves for Jackson's Island he is able to steal a whole ham, the loss of which is never noticed. When Tom and Becky are in the cave, they are constantly coming across subterranean springs and even discover a large lake. But, in the conclusion of the Injun Joe story, Twain makes a great point of how the murderer died of thirst as well as starvation.[6] And as we shall see, the characterization of Tom Sawyer is very uneven. His age is never specified, and it is difficult to picture him clearly. On Jackson's Island he acts like an eight-year-old, but in many of the scenes with Becky he seems closer to fourteen.

Twain also found it difficult to move from one story to another. When, for example, he wants to shift the scene from Jackson's Island back to St. Petersburg at the conclusion of chapter 16, he is forced to intrude rather awkwardly upon the text: "We will leave [the boys] to smoke and chatter and brag, since we have no further use for them at present." There is a large gap between chapter 24, which describes Tom's fear of Injun Joe, and chapter 25, which shows him cheerfully digging for treasure in a house he believes to be haunted. And Twain himself seems to realize that the conclusion to the novel is a bit abrupt, confessing, "When one writes a novel about grown people, he knows exactly where to stop—that is, with a marriage; but when he writes of juveniles, he must stop where he best can."

Nevertheless, there are a number of parallels among the various plots that help bind the work into a cohesive whole. The most obvious of these is that each of the principal adventures concerns a death—either real or supposed. One story begins with the death of Dr. Robinson, and another ends with the death of Injun

Joe. In the Jackson's Island episode, Tom pretends to be dead until he can enjoy a public triumph. And, in the cave sequence, Tom and Becky come very close to dying until—after three days—they rise from what might easily have been their tomb and return to town for the sort of joyful reunion that Tom has already experienced once before.

Moreover, the stories almost seem inevitable. They resolve themselves according to predictable patterns by drawing upon familiar myths, the most important of which are "the resurrection of the dead, the golden age, and the capture of the demon's hoard,"[7] as Robert Tracy has pointed out. Each of these myths is introduced as part of a game, but then realized by what actually comes to pass. The organization of the novel

depends in large part on a kind of thematic resonance or echo: a myth, a superstition, or an incident from romance is evoked, and this is followed by a sudden startling realization of that myth or romance. The boys pretend to be pirates and find themselves tracked by a murderer. They speculate about treasure according to Tom's half-baked romantic ideas, and behold, a treasure appears. The haunted house *is* haunted, by dangerous criminals. They dream of a "Delectable Land" of freedom, and with the Jackson's Island episode they really do sojourn in that land. Tom imagines situations in which he will die for Becky, and then finds himself in a situation in which he must truly act heroically to save her life. . . . Reality is continually interpenetrated by the mythic and the romantic worlds.[8]

But if much of *Tom Sawyer* has the familiarity of a fairy tale in which the hero ultimately wins the hand of a princess after a number of daring deeds, it also embodies another myth that is especially dear to the American heart. Among other things, it is a success story in which an orphan boy makes good, not through patience and industry, like Horatio Alger, but through imagination, self-reliance, and courage. Socially, Tom is not Becky's equal. He has only two sets of clothes, and there is an element of class antagonism in the enmity that immediately springs up between him and Alfred Temple, "that St. Louis smarty that thinks he dresses so fine and is aristocracy." (It is significant that after Tom and Becky quarrel, the judge's daughter chooses Alfred Temple as her new beau. A sneak who pours ink on Tom's spelling book, he is, at least, a member of her own class.) Tom may be "a bad, vicious, vulgar child," but he's got pluck, a virtue that Americans never fail to admire. His adventures all have one thing in common—they testify to his need for recognition. As Robert Regan has observed,

one element, motivation, unites all the actions. From first to last, young Thomas Sawyer, the orphan ward of a poor woman, a Sunday school scholar not noted for his studiousness, a frequent candidate for flogging in the regular school, and in every accepted sense a poor match for his younger brother, strives to win acceptance, admiration, love, and leadership, to win a place of some importance in his society.[9]

And as the book progresses, Tom is increasingly successful in achieving this goal. An early attempt to gain public recognition backfires when, after managing to pass himself off as the star pupil of his Sunday school class, he tells Judge Thatcher that the first two disciples were David and Goliath. But after this false step, he manages to do better. When he stages his own "death," his "fine joke" earns him temporary notoriety. When he testifies against Injun Joe in court, he becomes "a glittering hero once more—the pet of the old, the envy of the young." And when he not only leads Becky Thatcher out of the cave but unearths a fortune in gold, Tom fulfills his quest—he is "courted, admired, stared at" wherever he goes, and even his most casual remarks are "treasured and repeated." What child could ask for more?

It should thus be clear that episodic though it may be, *The Adventures of Tom Sawyer* is not without structure. While each of the adventures is a self-contained story, they ultimately come together to form a recognizable pattern. Not only do they parallel one another, they become increasingly serious, enabling the boy-hero to dominate those adults who were slow, at first, to recognize his true worth. Compared to *Life on the Mississippi,* there is relatively little extraneous material. And when we remember that *Tom Sawyer* anticipates that work by several years, we should recognize that its construction is relatively sophisticated.

Twain saw his book as "intended mainly for the entertainment of boys and girls," but he hoped that it would not be "shunned by men and women on that account, for part of my plan has been to pleasantly remind adults of what they once were themselves, and of how they felt and thought and talked, and what queer enterprises they sometimes engaged in." But the modern reader is apt to feel that childhood was never quite so idyllic as pictured here. The vision of childhood offered in these pages is very much an adult vision, determined at least in part by the sentimental distortions of memory. For all his professed scorn of romanticism, Twain helped further the romantic myth of the child as a wonderfully inventive free spirit who is infinitely superior to the adult world in which he is forced to dwell.

Ironically, Twain's original purpose was to present a realistic picture of childhood. Nineteenth-century children's books tended to celebrate impossibly industrious and noble-hearted lads who always ate their spinach and never told a lie. Within such texts, the mischievous were routinely punished, leading youthful readers to believe that anyone who smoked a cigarette at the age of twelve was certain to end his days as a drunken beggar, his survival dependent upon alms supplied by his studious and well-behaved classmates, now risen to the glory of managing a bank or running a newspaper. Twain rebelled against this, recognizing that observation does not bear out the idea that life rewards the virtuous—if "virtue" can be defined in such narrow terms.[10]

The point of view that we find here is suggested by a passage from *Life on the Mississippi*:

If the Model Boy was in either of these Sunday schools, I did not see him. The Model Boy of my time—we never had but one—was perfect; perfect in dress, perfect in conduct, perfect in filial piety, perfect in exterior godliness; but at bottom he was a prig; and as for the contents of his skull, they could have changed place with the contents of a pie and nobody would have been the worse off for it but the pie. The fellow's reproachlessness was a standing reproach to every lad in the village. He was the admiration of all the mothers, and the detestation of all their sons.

One of the first things we are told about Tom is that "He was not the Model Boy of the village. He knew the model boy very well though—and he loathed him." Within the first few chapters, he lies, fights, and steals; plays hooky, and cons other boys into doing his work for him. But as his characterization develops, he begins to emerge as simply a variation of the Model Boy, a new "model" so to speak. He is mischievous, but his mischief is looked upon as proof of his incipient masculinity. Twain seems to believe that this is "what a normal boy should be," his shenanigans but "a harmless part of his maturing."[11] We are encouraged to subscribe to the dubious notion that "boys will be boys"—a type of sexual stereotyping that defines hostility to school and running away from home as perfectly acceptable behavior if one is to grow into a man capable of seizing Panama and storming San Juan Hill.[12]

In keeping with this characterization, we are told

that Tom loathes getting dressed in his Sunday clothes. Although he is presented to us as a show-off who loves nothing so much as having the eyes of the village upon him, he does not like to dress up. On the contrary, "there was a restraint about whole clothes and cleanliness that galled him." He leaves that sort of thing to girls—or sissies, like his half-brother, Sid. For his own part, he is too busy to worry about the state of his fingernails. Indeed, at times he seems almost hyperactive. Consider how he amuses himself in the schoolyard:

The next moment he was out, and "going on" like an Indian; yelling, laughing, chasing boys, jumping over the fence at risk of life and limb, throwing handsprings, standing on his head—doing all the heroic things he could conceive of . . . he came war-whooping around, snatched a boy's cap, hurled it to the roof of the school-house, broke through a group of boys, tumbling them in every direction, and fell sprawling, himself, under Becky's nose.

Adults might think such antics are cute, but they're not the ones being knocked over or having their hat snatched. The actual victims of his aggression probably welcomed the days on which Tom chose to stay away from school.

Although seemingly at odds with St. Petersburg propriety, Tom Sawyer is really only a weekend rebel. He is more interested in dominating the schoolyard than in withdrawing from it. His strongest instincts are for his own self-advancement. A rudimentary capitalist, he trades refuse for enough tickets to earn a prize Bible, and in the most famous scene in the novel, he tricks his friends into paying him for the privilege of whitewashing Aunt Polly's fence. He is, in short, a juvenile version of the con-men who populate *Life on the Mississippi*, a pint-size Hank Morgan addicted to power, profits, and prestige—none of which can be realized for long on Jackson's Island.[13] Tom needs St.

Petersburg for his modus vivendi. The town provides the "eager auditory" upon which he depends. And so it is perfectly in character for him to bribe Huck Finn, at the conclusion of the novel, into conforming with local mores: "We can't let you into the gang if you ain't respectable, you know."

It thus follows that Tom is relatively predictable even when he is being "adventurous"; he is not a genuinely imaginative child. Almost all of his ideas come from books. For a boy who hates to do his homework, he has read a good deal of romantic fiction, and he insists that his various escapades conform to literary models—"the authorities," as he calls them. When playing at being Robin Hood, he demands that his friend Joe Harper fall to the ground as if he had been slain. The two boys had been pretending to fence, and Joe protests, "I shan't! Why don't you fall yourself? You're getting the worst of it." And Tom responds with what he considers an irrefutable argument:

Why, that ain't anything. *I* can't fall; that ain't the way it is in the book. The book says, "Then with one backhanded stroke he slew poor Guy of Guisborne." You're to turn around and let me hit you in the back.

Tom is allowed to have his way, not because he deserves to win the game but because he claims to be backed by the respectability of tradition: "There was no getting around the authorities, so Joe turned, received the whack, and fell."

In a parallel scene, Tom explains to Huck the advantages of being a pirate as opposed to being a hermit—two roles that had come to fascinate him from his reading. Huck, however, is a refreshingly skeptical audience:

"You see," said Tom, "people don't go much on hermits, nowadays, like they used to in old times, but a pirate's always respected. And a hermit's got to sleep on the hardest place he can find, and put sackcloth and ashes on his head, and stand out in the rain, and—"

"What does he put sackcloth and ashes on his head for?" inquired Huck.

"*I* dono. But they've *got* to do it. Hermits always do. You'd have to do that if you want to be a hermit."

"Derned if I would," said Huck.

"Well, what would you do?"

"I dunno. But I wouldn't do that."

"Why, Huck, you'd *have* to. How'd you get around it?"

"Why, I just wouldn't stand it. I'd run away."

"Run away! Well you *would* be a nice old slouch of a hermit. You'd be a disgrace."

Huck allows the argument to drop at this point so that he can smoke his corn cob pipe "in the full bloom of luxurious contentment." Characteristically, Tom envies Huck for possessing "this majestic vice." He likes the idea of smoking, but when he actually tries it, the experience makes him sick.

As the dialogue quoted above suggests, Huck Finn is a far more interesting character than Tom Sawyer. His determination to "run away" rather than conform to alien customs foreshadows precisely what he will do in the book devoted to his own adventures. Within *The Adventures of Tom Sawyer*, however, he serves primarily as a foil to Tom. Like "the rest of the respectable boys," Tom admires Huck because he is "the only boy in town who is completely free." Of course no one is ever "completely free"—not even Huck, who is frequently dominated by the powerful personality of his friend. But compared to Tom, Huck seems to be in control of his own life.

Huckleberry came and went, at his own free will. He slept on doorsteps in fine weather and in empty hogsheads in wet; he did not have to go to school or to church, or call any being master or obey anybody; he could go fishing or swimming when and where he chose, and stay as long as it suited him; nobody forbade him to fight; he could sit up as late as he pleased; he was always the first boy that went barefoot in the spring and the last to resume leather in the fall; he never had to wash, nor put on clean clothes; he could swear wonderfully. In a word, everything that goes to make life precious that boy had. So thought every harassed, hampered, respectable boy in St. Petersburg.

Tom Sawyer is unquestionably one of the harassed and hampered who envy Huck. But it is difficult to believe that he is ill-used by the kindly Aunt Polly— or, for that matter, by any of the other adults in town. Aunt Polly seems capable of forgiving Tom almost anything. As she explains in the opening chapter, "He's full of the Old Scratch, but laws-a-me! he's my own dead sister's boy, poor thing, and I ain't got the heart to lash him, somehow." And there is nothing very imposing about the other figures of authority with whom Tom must contend. The doctor gets murdered, the minister is upstaged by a beetle, and the schoolmaster is exposed as a fraud. The Widow Douglas seems ever ready to dish out ice cream and new sets of clothes. And Judge Thatcher virtually adopts Tom at the end of the novel.

Indeed, St. Petersburg as a whole seems extraordinarily charitable toward Tom. He makes everyone look ridiculous by staging his own death, but when he shows up at his funeral, he is received with unaffected joy:

Suddenly the minister shouted at the top of his voice: "Praise God from whom all blessings flow—SING!—and put your hearts in it!"

And they did. "Old Hundred" swelled up with a triumphant burst, and while it shook the rafters Tom Sawyer the Pirate looked around upon the envying juveniles about him and confessed in his heart that this was the proudest moment of his life.

As the "sold" congregation trooped out they said they would almost be willing to be made ridiculous again to hear "Old Hundred" sung like that once more.

The significance of this scene should not be overlooked by readers who like to believe that Twain uncritically admired life on an island—or a raft—at the expense of the American small town. Tom is welcomed back into a community remarkable for its harmony. As Henry Nash Smith has persuasively argued, "The official culture of St. Petersburg could hardly receive a more absolute affirmation."[14]

So who then is responsible for harassing Tom? And the answer is Tom himself. He is harassed by his all-consuming ambition to achieve personal distinction. He is desperate to succeed, and as a result, even his games tend to be carefully regimented. He may envy Huck, but he would never imitate him for long. Nothing makes him happier than to have a church full of people singing a Te Deum over him, and he'd never be able to hear it in a hogshead.

And if Tom is "hampered" as well as harassed, it is because he is incapable of learning from experience. He may be successful at the end of his adventures—in terms of fortune and social status. But he is not a whit the wiser. Although some critics hold that *The Adventures of Tom Sawyer* chronicles Tom's progress from childhood to maturity,[15] the evidence suggests otherwise. One might expect his experience at Muff Potter's trial to have been at least a little sobering, but afterward Tom still likes to play at being a robber. He is later given much credit for leading Becky out of the cave, but it should be remembered that he is responsible for getting them lost in the first place. After making it back to safety, he reveals that his juvenile egotism remains intact. When he tells others about this adventure, he puts in "many striking additions to adorn it withal." He then promises to give Huck his drum in order to entice him into exploring the cave. And as they approach the secret entrance that Tom had discovered, his values are indistinguishable from those he had expressed on Jackson's Island. Life is still a game:

"Here you are! Look at it, Huck; it's the snuggest hole in this country. You just keep mum about it. All along I've been wanting to be a robber, but I knew I'd got to have a thing like this, and where to run across it was the bother. We've got it now, and we'll keep it quiet, only we'll let Joe Harper and Ben Rogers in—because of course there's got to be a gang, or else there wouldn't be any style about it. Tom Sawyer's Gang—it sounds splendid, don't it, Huck?"

"Well, it just does, Tom. And who'll we rob?"

"Oh, most anybody. Waylay people—that's mostly the way."

"And kill them?"

"No, not always. Hide them in a cave till they raise a ransom."

"What's a ransom?"

"Money. You make them raise all they can, off'n their friends; and after you've kept them a year, if it ain't raised then you kill them. That's the general way. . . . It's so in all the books."

"Why, it's real bully, Tom. I b'lieve it's better'n to be a pirate."

Yes, it's better in some ways, because it's close to home and circuses and all that."

Despite his own close encounters with death, Tom still likes to think that murder is cute. Like robbery and extortion, it is part of the fantasy life to which he consistently clings. At the conclusion of the novel, we leave him explaining to Huck what it means to be initiated into his gang: "It's to swear to stand by one another, and never tell the gang's secrets, even if you're chopped all to flinders, and kill anybody and all his family that hurts one of the gang." The ceremony, as he envisions it, will involve signing an oath in blood—

on a coffin, at midnight. Such plans as these do not evince a mature point of view. As Twain himself reminds us in his epilogue, the book is "strictly a history of a *boy*."

But this does not mean that we are meant to dismiss Tom lightly. If thoughtful readers find him tiresome, it is because we are beginning to escape from the sentimental stereotypes in which the nineteenth century enveloped children. Tom may be the occasional victim of Twain's irony, especially in those scenes in which he shows a naive enthusiasm for romantic fiction, but he is presented sympathetically for the most part. Generations of readers have found him to be the archetypal American boy—ingenuous and cute, but reassuringly bold and aggressive. Realistic or not, he continues to be esteemed by those adults who are anxious to believe that children are entertaining and that their games are nothing more than "good clean fun."

An intelligent reader does not judge a book by the extent to which he can sympathize with the protagonist. One cannot judge *The Adventures of Tom Sawyer* simply in terms of whether or not one shares Twain's affection for Tom. If it is to be faulted as a work of art, it is not on the grounds of its characterization so much as its diction. Writing to William Dean Howells shortly after he had finished the book, Twain confessed that he had "perhaps made a mistake in not writing it in the first person."[16] In *The Adventures of Huckleberry Finn*, which he would write over the next decade, much of the work's power can be traced to the fact that the narration comes to us as if directly from Huck, and the idiom of a poorly educated but intelligent boy gives to the novel not only originality but, more importantly, verisimilitude. In *Tom Sawyer*, however, Twain had yet to make this breakthrough. The story is told in the third person—an adult, in New England, far removed from his material. Thus despite the book's sympathy with juvenile horseplay, the diction often seems more appropriate to a Victorian parlor than secret camps on the fringe of the American frontier. Consider, for example, the following passage:

He wandered far from the accustomed haunts of boys, and sought desolate places that were in harmony with his spirit. A log raft in the river invited him, and he seated himself on its outer edge and contemplated the dreary vastness of the stream, wishing, the while, that he could be drowned, all at once, and unconsciously, without undergoing the uncomfortable routine devised by nature.

We might well be reading James Fenimore Cooper.[17] One could argue that the language in question here is intended ironically, as a means of satirizing Tom's rather stagy melancholia. But while this case might be made for phrases like "the dreary vastness of the stream," phrases that serve only to further the action are equally verbose. There's no reason why Tom couldn't simply see a log and sit down on it. Instead, we have him "invited" to sit on "its outer edge," as if Tom is worried about getting dirt on his clothes. The language is altogether too proper; it conveys a visual image of someone with careful manners even in the wild, which is not the way we have been led to see Tom. Language becomes a barrier between subject and reader, preventing Twain's audience from entering a Missouri childhood as if it were their own.

Twain is especially florid when he writes about the natural world that draws the boys away from town. He likes to tidy things up, giving "outer edges" to logs and leaving out the mosquitoes that probably filled the air. Nature becomes an idealized landscape. On Jackson's Island, Tom and Huck "tramped gaily along . . . among the solemn monarchs of the forest, hung from their crowns to the ground with a drooping regalia of grape-vines. Now and then they came upon snug nooks carpeted with grass and jeweled with flowers." Self-consciously picturesque, such language as this makes the island seem nothing more than an extension of the town—the St. Petersburg Botanical Garden, as it were. It follows, therefore, that the boys "found plenty of things to be delighted with, but nothing to be astonished at." The frontier has been turned into the countryside, the sublime into the pretty—a nonthreatening background perfectly suitable for picnics.

The diction occasionally suggests that Twain was not writing "mainly for the entertainment of boys and girls" but for their parents.[18] When Tom climbs in through a window after being out for much of the night, "he uncovered an ambuscade, in the person of his aunt . . . her resolution to turn his Saturday holiday into captivity at hard labor became adamantine in its firmness." Few children are likely to include "adamantine" in their vocabulary, and there is no reason why Twain could not have had Tom ambushed by his aunt as opposed to making him uncover an "ambuscade." The style sometimes even seems to patronize children. Seen from a distance, there is something comic even about their suffering. In one scene, Aunt Polly removes a tooth from Tom's mouth by a process that involves thrusting a burning log in his face. But Twain is quick to reassure us:

As Tom wended to school after breakfast, he was the envy of every boy he met because the gap in his upper row of teeth enabled him to expectorate in a new and admirable way. He gathered quite a following of lads interested in the exhibition; and one that had cut his finger and been a center of fascination and homage up to this time now found himself suddenly without an adherent, and shorn of his glory.

There is a certain undefinable smugness to passages like this, conveyed not only by the artificiality of words like "wended" and "expectorate" but also by the author's blithe assumption that wounds don't hurt, that lost teeth and cut fingers are cute when contrasted with the problems of adults. Childish woes may seem ridiculous to someone who is quarreling with his publisher and worried about his investments, but that does not mean they are not felt keenly by the children themselves. Unfortunately, very little sense of this comes across in *Tom Sawyer* because Twain's style is too often at odds with the subject matter.

Modern readers are also likely to take exception to the racism that pervades the book. Because St. Petersburg is basically at harmony with itself, the villain has to be an outsider.[19] But everyone knows Injun Joe; he is an outsider simply because of his race. Just before killing Dr. Robinson the "half-breed" declares, "The Injun blood ain't in me for nothing." And later, when he plans to attack the Widow Douglas, Huck is afraid to reveal his identity, describing him as a Spaniard since that was how Injun Joe had disguised himself. The man who comes to Huck's assistance observes that Huck is holding something back, prompting the boy to confess, "'Tain't a Spaniard—it's Injun Joe!" And this, it seems, explains everything:

It's all plain enough, now. When you talked about notching ears and slitting noses I judged that was your own embellishment, because white men don't take that sort of revenge. But an Injun! That's a different matter altogether.

And if Indians are mean and treacherous, blacks are comic and lazy. A slave named Jim, destined to become a principal character in *Huckleberry Finn*, appears here in only one scene. Illustrating the wonderful sense of rhythm that blacks are supposed to possess, "Jim came skipping out at the gate with a tin pail, and singing 'Buffalo Gals.'" He is en route to the town pump, and "although the pump was only a hundred and fifty yards off, Jim never got back with a bucket of water under an hour—and even then somebody generally had to go after him."

It should be recognized, however, that Twain's position is more complex than it may seem at first. He is careful to establish a motive for Injun Joe's crimes. The Indian reminds Dr. Robinson that he had once driven him from his door:

Five years ago you drove me away from your father's kitchen one night, when I come to ask for something to eat, and you said I warn't there for any good; and when I swore I'd get even with you if it took a hundred years, your father had me jailed for a vagrant. Did you think I'd forget?

And his attack upon the Widow Douglas springs from another instance of mistreatment. Her husband

was rough on me—many times he was rough on me—and mainly he was the justice of the peace that jugged me for a vagrant. And that ain't all. It ain't a millionth part of it! He had me *horsewhipped!*—horsewhipped in front of the jail, like a nigger!—with all the town looking on! HORSE-WHIPPED!—do you understand?

So it is possible to argue that Injun Joe is "a figure whose evil has been provoked by white injustice."[20] And the comic portrayal of Jim should be measured against what Huck says about another slave:

I tote water for Uncle Jake whenever he wants me to, and any time I ask him he gives me a little something to eat if he can spare it. That's a mighty good nigger, Tom. He likes me becuz I don't ever act as if I was above him. Sometimes I've set right down and eat *with* him. But you needn't tell that. A body's got to do things when he's awful hungry he wouldn't want to do as a steady thing.

The parallel here with Dr. Robinson's father is worth noting: The white man drives a beggar away from his kitchen, while the black man shares the little food he has.

It would be fair to say that *Tom Sawyer* reveals the first signs of Twain's interest in race as a social problem. But too much should not be made of this. Blacks are so incidental to the story that the novel could almost be set in Minnesota. And relatively little sympathy is wasted on Injun Joe. He is unquestionably villainous, and we are certainly meant to rejoice at his death. Moreover, both Injun Joe and Huck share the prevailing outlook in the town on questions of race. The Indian is offended that he was treated "like a nigger," and Huck is ashamed of himself for having sat down to eat with a slave.

It would be unfair, of course, to condemn a work because it reflects the sociological values of its own time and fails to anticipate the views we now hold. But, when compared to the great sequel that followed it, *The Adventures of Tom Sawyer* is more dated. It is flawed by Twain's inability to free himself from the rhetorical flourishes of nineteenth-century prose. And compared to Twain's later works, it seems a bit complacent, too readily endorsing stereotypical notions of childhood, class, and race.

Whatever its limitations, *Tom Sawyer* remains one of the most popular of Twain's works. A book in which dreams come true, it tells us—for the most part—what we want to hear, satisfying "some need at the very taproot of American life."[21] Nonetheless, there are hints within it that foreshadow the anger and despair that would come to dominate Twain's subsequent work.

For all of its charm, St. Petersburg is still a "little shabby village" haunted by the same sense of loneliness and isolation we found in *Life on the Mississippi*. The graveyard, for example, is a vision of decay:

Grass and weeds grew rank over the whole cemetary. All the old graves were sunken in, there was not a tombstone on the place; round-topped, worm-eaten boards staggered over the graves, leaning for support and finding none.

And a later scene takes place in an abandoned house in which "there was something so weird and grisly about the dead silence that reigned under the baking sun, and something so depressing about the loneliness and desolation of the place, that they were afraid, for a moment, to venture in." It's reasonable, of course, to expect graveyards and old empty houses to be at least a little bleak, but we find the same note of deathlike solitude even in the midst of nature:

There was not even a zephyr stirring; the dead noonday heat had even stilled the songs of the birds; nature lay in a trance that was broken by no sound but the occasional far-off hammering of a woodpecker, and this seemed to render the pervading silence and sense of loneliness the more profound.

Nature seems only to emphasize the isolation that Tom is feeling when he goes to the river for comfort. And during the celebrated interlude on Jackson's Island, Joe Harper gets "so homesick that he could hardly endure the misery of it." Huck becomes "melancholy" and Tom "downhearted," afflicted by "mutinous depression." Joe actually prepares to leave the island, and Huck tries to go with him, observing that "It was getting so lonesome anyway, and now it'll be worse." Tom is forced to use all his ingenuity in order to keep his friends with him. He succeeds, but toward the end of their stay, "the dull dead heat of the breathless atmosphere was stifling."

This is nothing, however, compared to the isolation Tom and Becky experience in the cave, the cave in which Injun Joe is ultimately entombed. Already cut off from the town because of his race, he finds himself utterly alone and gradually starves to death. This is, as we have seen, only one of the deaths in the novel, but metaphorically, it is especially significant. Moreover, it gives Twain the occasion to introduce what would eventually become one of his favorite themes, the fickle foolishness of the average man:

Injun Joe was buried near the mouth of the cave; and people flocked there in boats and wagons from the towns and from all the farms and hamlets for seven miles around; they brought their children, and all sorts of provisions, and confessed that they had had almost as satisfactory a time at the funeral as they could have had at the hanging.

This funeral stopped the further growth of one thing—the petition to the governor for Injun Joe's pardon. The petition had been largely signed; and many tearful and eloquent meetings had been held, and a committee of sappy women been appointed to go in deep mourning and wail around the governor, and implore him to be a merciful ass and trample his duty underfoot. Injun Joe was believed to have killed five citizens of the village, but what of that? If he been Satan himself there would have been plenty of weaklings ready to scribble their names to a pardon petition, and drip a tear on it from their permanently impaired and leaky waterworks.

The cynicism of this passage borders on contempt, and it is hard to justify in a work "intended mainly for the entertainment of boys and girls." But the citizens of St. Petersburg will prove to have much in common with the inhabitants of Bricksville, Camelot, and Dawson's Landing—the "small towns" of Twain's later works.

Twain could not abide cant, and his attack upon the "committee of sappy women" is only one of several instances in which he ridicules insincerity. When Muff Potter is proved innocent of the Robinson murder, Twain dryly observes that "the fickle, unreasoning world took Muff Potter to its bosom and fondled him as lavishly as it had abused him before." And several scenes are devoted to satirizing religious hypocrisy. The great event of the St. Petersburg school year is "Examination Evening," at which the children

are expected to recite carefully memorized speeches.
Twain objects to these compositions for a number of
reasons, but he is particularly offended by

the inveterate and intolerable sermon that wagged its
crippled tail at the end of each and every one of them. No
matter what the subject might be, a brain-racking effort was
made to squirm it into some aspect or other that the moral
and religious mind could contemplate with edification. The
glaring insincerity of these sermons was not sufficient to
compass their banishment from the schools. . . . and you
will find that the sermon of the most frivolous and the least
religious girl in the school is always the longest and the most
relentlessly pious.

One such speech is "so destructive of all hope to non-
Presbyterians that it took first prize," and this establishes a link to the town's minister. When we follow
Tom to church on Sunday, we are treated to a sermon
"that dealt in limitless fire and brimstone and thinned
the predestined elect down to a company so small as to
be hardly worth the saving." There is good reason,
however, to question the depth of the minister's faith.
He prays for "the poor sailors, tossed by stormy seas,"
and "the oppressed millions groaning under the heel of
European monarchies and Oriental despotisms"—
copybook phrases that could have had little meaning
in rural Missouri. Ignoring most of what he has to say,
his congregation occasionally responds to the way he
says it, believing him to be "a wonderful reader":

At church "sociables" he was always called upon to read
poetry, and when he was through, the ladies would lift up
their hands and let them fall helplessly in their laps, and
"wall" their eyes, and shake their heads, as much to say,
"Words cannot express it; it is too beautiful, *too* beautiful for
this mortal earth."

Their enthusiasm seems too ritualized to be genuine,
and the poetry itself even less important than the dec-

lamation. Like Tom, they value style to excess, a harmless vice, perhaps, except that the ladies who "wall"
their eyes over poetry later become the women who
are always ready to "drip a tear . . . from their permanently impaired and leaky waterworks," in order to
persuade the governor to be "a merciful ass."

   Twain's satire of public piety leads him to ridicule
"conscience," a subject on which he would elaborate in
A Connecticut Yankee in King Arthur's Court and *The
Mysterious Stranger*, among other works. When Muff
Potter is wrongfully imprisoned, Tom goes to the jail
every few days and smuggles "such small comforts . . .
as he could get hold of" in through the grated window.
Tom has it in his power to set Muff Potter free, but he
doesn't do so until much later because "These offer-
ings greatly helped to ease Tom's conscience." A conscience must be a paltry thing if it can be appeased so
easily by sentimental gestures. But, foolish though it
may be, it can also be exasperating. After the boys run
away to Jackson's Island, they have trouble sleeping
because they feel guilty about having stolen provisions
from home. And Twain seems to find something
comic in their guilt:

It was conscience. They began to feel a vague fear that they
had been doing wrong to run away; and next they thought of
the stolen meat, and then the real torture came. They tried to
argue it away by reminding conscience that they had pur-
loined sweetmeats and apples scores of times; but conscience was not to be appeased by such thin plausibilities; it
seemed to them in the end, that there was no getting around
the stubborn fact that taking sweetmeats was only "hook-
ing," while taking bacon and hams and such valuables was
plain simple *stealing*—and there was a command against that
in the Bible.

While not an overt attack upon conscience, the passage
tends to make moral scruples seem ridiculous. Our

conscience regularly allows us to commit venial sins, and then it suddenly flares up—when we are trying to sleep—after we have done something that is only the logical extension of the moral compromises we make every day.

And finally, even Twain's eventual fascination with determinist philosophy can be found within the pages of this seemingly simple book. Desperate for water, Injun Joe had found a small measure of relief in a drip from the roof of the cave that yielded "a dessert-spoonful one in every four and twenty hours." This leads Twain to reflect:

Has everything a purpose and a mission? Did this drop fall patiently during five thousand years to be ready for this flit-ting human insect's need? And has it another important ob-ject to accomplish ten thousand years to come?

This type of speculation has nothing to do with either his narrative or his audience. That he indulges in it is a sign that he could not be content for long with writing for children.

One of the most undervalued works of American fiction—by critics, if not by readers—*Tom Sawyer* suffers from the inevitable comparison with *Huckle-berry Finn*. But like *Huck*, it can be read on a number of levels. Adults who reread the book are almost al-ways struck by how there is much more to it than a child is likely to grasp. At the time of its publication, Twain's greatest works were still before him. But *The Adventures of Tom Sawyer* points the way to the rest of his career.

4

ᴕᴕ

An American Odyssey:
The Adventures of Huckleberry Finn

It took Mark Twain over seven years to write *The Adventures of Huckleberry Finn*, and it initially met with a mixed reception, rejected in some quarters as "rough, coarse and inelegant . . . more suited to the slums than to intelligent, respectable people."[1] But within Twain's lifetime, *Huckleberry Finn* became the most remunerative of all his works, and it has since established itself as an American classic. Praised by T. S. Eliot, celebrated by Ernest Hemingway, and recommended by thousands of high school English teachers, Twain's finest novel now carries the burden of so much criticism that the work itself threatens to become lost amid the almost endless volumes devoted to its explication.

There can be no question that *Huckleberry Finn* has become "one of the central documents of American culture."[2] A book that can delight both fourteen-year-olds and graduate professors of literature is rare indeed, and we should give it careful attention. But we should not approach it with exaggerated reverence. Surely Twain himself, who devoted so much of his energy to satirizing cultural institutions, would find it ironic if we did so.

The novel is set in the Mississippi River valley, "forty to fifty years ago" according to the original title page of 1885. The story is told directly by Huck, and it begins shortly after *Tom Sawyer* left off. Huck has been living with the Widow Douglas and her sister, Miss Watson, an experience that has left him feeling "all cramped up." Accustomed to being "free and easy," he cannot abide life within this well-regulated household, where he is expected to sit up straight, do his homework, and pray to a God he cannot see. Within a few pages of the opening chapter, Huck is already yearning for adventure. "All I wanted was to go somewheres," he tells us, "all I wanted was a change, I warn't particular."

Change soon appears in the person of Huck's father, Pap Finn, previously believed to be dead. When he goes to his room one night, Huck finds his father waiting for him, and his description of the man makes it clear that he is far removed from the world of clean sheets and spelling books in which Huck has recently been living.

He was most fifty, and he looked it. His hair was long and tangled and greasy, and hung down, and you could see his eyes shining through like he was behind vines. . . . There warn't no color in his face, where his face showed; it was white; not like another man's white, but a white to make a body sick, a white to make a body's flesh crawl—a tree-toad white, a fish-belly white.

Grotesque though he may seem, and brutal as he will soon prove himself to be, there can be no question that this is Huck's father. All the images used to describe him spring from the natural world to which Huck yearns to return.

Pap wants the six thousand dollars in gold that had come to Huck at the end of *Tom Sawyer,* money that has been invested, in Huck's behalf, by Judge Thatcher. Having claimed his son and brought suit to obtain his fortune, Pap takes Huck to a cabin in the woods and keeps him there as a prisoner, locking him in for as long as three days at a time while he goes off to town to get drunk. At first, Huck actually enjoys his life with Pap:

It was kind of lazy and jolly, laying off comfortable all day smoking and fishing, and no books nor study. Two months or more run along, and my clothes got to be all rags and dirt, and I didn't see how I'd ever got to like it so well at the widow's, where you had to wash, and eat on a plate. . . . I didn't want to go back no more. . . . It was pretty good times up in the woods there, take it all around.

But Pap suffers from delirium tremens, and during one of his fits he attacks Huck with a knife. Huck is convinced that he cannot continue to live with his father, and he plans a clever escape.

When his father is away in town, Huck cuts a hole in the back of the wooden cabin. He crawls outside and then reinserts the log he had cut out, disguising the rough edges with rocks and dust. He then goes hunting and shoots a wild pig which he brings back to the cabin. Smashing down the front door, he cuts the pig's throat and lets it bleed on the earthen floor. He also bloodies the ax and attaches some of his own hair to it. After disposing of the pig and laying a false trail, Huck makes for the river—and a canoe he had kept hidden on the shore. He has staged his own "murder" so that no one will come looking for him.

His destination is Jackson's Island, about two and a half miles downstream from St. Petersburg. He sets up camp there and, carefully hidden, watches as the townspeople search the river for his body. After three days on the island, he discovers that Miss Watson's Jim, a Negro slave, has also sought refuge on the island, convinced that he was about to be sold downriver. The boy and the man become allies.

Huck sneaks ashore one night and discovers that the island is about to be searched by men hoping to recapture Jim. He hurries back to warn Jim, "There ain't a minute to lose. They're after us!" Quickly gathering together their few supplies, Huck and Jim escape on a raft that they had caught a few days earlier as it had drifted by the island.

The next several chapters are often regarded as the heart of the novel. They trace the growing relationship between Huck and Jim as they float down the Mississippi, ostensibly to freedom. They plan to go only so far as Cairo, Illinois, where the Mississippi joins the Ohio—a point at which Jim should be able to secure passage into free territory.

Unfortunately, they can travel only at night for fear of being picked up, and they miss Cairo in a fog. Shortly afterward, the raft is run into by a steamboat. Jim and Huck jump overboard at the last minute, and Huck dives for the bottom of the river "for a thirty-foot wheel had got to go over me, and I wanted to have plenty of room." When he comes up for air, he calls for Jim without getting any answer. Convinced that Jim is dead, he makes his way to shore.

Calling himself George Jackson, Huck is taken in by Col. Grangerford and his family, local southern gentry. The Grangerfords seem thoroughly admirable—except for their devotion to a long-standing feud with another prominent family, the Shepherdsons. Within the next two chapters, Huck sees Col. Grangerford and his three sons killed in the feud. He flees back to the river—and to Jim, who now reappears in the story; he had been afraid to call out to Huck in the river the night of their accident for fear that he might be discovered by someone who would sell him back into slavery. During the days Huck has spent with the Grangerfords, Jim has been busy repairing the raft, and they are therefore able to continue their journey south.

For the next few days, Huck and Jim drift down the river, experiencing what has become the archetypal

American idyll. Huck tells us that "we let the raft alone, and let her float wherever the current wanted to; then we lit the pipes, and dangled our legs in the water and talked about all kinds of things." But on a brief excursion to the shore, Huck encounters two scoundrels who are being run out of a nearby town. The "duke" and the "king," as they call themselves, beg to be taken on board the raft. Both Jim and Huck are naturally compassionate, and they not only take the men on board but allow them to take charge of the raft as if it were their own.

As this unlikely crew of four make their way into the Deep South, they stop at various small towns along the shore, allowing Twain to portray a wide range of American life in the first half of the nineteenth century. Prominent among these towns is Bricksville, where Huck sees a man shot down in cold blood, an incident based upon Twain's own experience as a boy. The people of this town are thoroughly disagreeable. Huck tells us that nothing could "wake them up all over, and make them happy all over, like a dog-fight—unless it might be putting turpentine on a stray dog and setting fire to him, or tying a tin pan to his tail and see him run himself to death." The king and the duke exploit this unsavory lot by offering *The Royal Nonesuch*—a performance that involves nothing but the king prancing about naked as if he were an animal. Provocatively advertised, *The Royal Nonesuch* draws a large crowd for three nights.[3]

But this playacting is only a prelude to greater deceit. In a town further down the river, the king discovers that a prominent citizen has died, leaving his money to a brother who no one in the town has ever met. The king pretends to be the brother of the deceased and comes alarmingly close to making off with all the dead man's wealth, leaving his legitimate heirs impoverished. Huck records that "It was enough to make a body ashamed of the human race," and he risks the king's wrath to help foil the plan.

But the king and the duke now work their meanest deal. They have handbills printed describing Jim as a runaway slave from a plantation near New Orleans, and the king then reveals where Jim can be found. Jim is recaptured and imprisoned on a nearby farm. This precipitates a crisis of conscience for Huck. He believes that his moral duty is to write to Miss Watson and tell her where she can find her "runaway nigger." But he can't bring himself to do it. He remembers all the experiences he has shared with Jim, and by listening to his heart rather than to his conscience, he decides to help Jim escape from his captors in a scene that is usually considered the climax of the novel. Huck believes that to steal Jim out of slavery is a sin, but he must still do what he feels is right, regardless of the consequences. In his resolution, he boldly declares, "All right, then I'll go to hell."

The next ten chapters are devoted to rescuing Jim, and these are the chapters that have inspired most of the controversy surrounding the novel. Through the sort of coincidence seldom seen outside the nineteenth-century novel, it emerges that Jim is held captive by none other than Tom Sawyer's Aunt Sally and Uncle Silas Phelps, who—at the moment Huck arrives at their door—are expecting a visit from the nephew they have never seen. Huck pretends to be Tom. And tipped off by Huck, who has met him on the road, Tom pretends to be his own brother Sid. Tom agrees to help Huck rescue Jim, but he quickly takes charge of the whole operation and turns it into an elaborate adventure in imitation of the romantic fiction he loves to read. Jim's cabin is deliberately infested with snakes and rats, for example, and Tom makes Jim keep a journal in blood on a shirt stolen from Aunt Sally's clothesline. Although it would have been possible to free Jim easily from his unguarded cabin within a few hours, the boys turn the job into an escapade that lasts for weeks.

When Jim is finally freed, he gets no further than the river. The victim of his own theatrics, Tom is shot in the leg by a farmer, and Jim will not abandon the wounded boy, who soon becomes delirious. As the result of his fidelity, Jim is recaptured and put in chains. But when Tom Sawyer recovers, he makes the surprising announcement that Jim has been a free man for months: Miss Watson had died and set him free in her will. Tom pays Jim forty dollars to compensate him "for being a prisoner . . . so patient, and doing it up so good."[4] And the novel closes with Huck's often quoted promise "to light out for the Territory . . . because Aunt Sally she's going to adopt me and sivilize me and I can't stand it. I been there before."

Many readers feel disappointed by the conclusion of *Huckleberry Finn*, finding it contrived, unconvincing, and antithetical to the spirit of the novel as a whole. Bernard DeVoto complained that "in the whole reach of the English novel there is no more abrupt or chilling descent."[5] More recent critics have dismissed the conclusion as a "travesty"[6] and "a failure of nerve."[7] As Walter Blair has explained:

The chief crimes are against characterization: Jim, whom the reader and Huck have come to love and admire, becomes a victim of meaningless torture, a cartoon. Huck, who has fought against codes of civilization, follows one of the silliest of them.

And he speculates that "perhaps even the ebullient Mark Twain was tired to the point of reckless improvisation."[8]

Other critics, most notably Lionel Trilling and T. S. Eliot, have defended the conclusion on the grounds that it has "a certain formal aptness"[9] that enables Twain to restate his primary concerns in another key and "beat his way back from incipient tragedy to the comic resolution called for in the original conception of the story."[10] But this approach emphasizes the structure of the novel, and as Leo Marx has observed, "Structure . . . is only one element—indeed, one of the more mechanical elements of unity."[11]

I believe that the conclusion can be defended in the very area where it seems the most vulnerable—characterization. If the final chapters of the novel seem to divest both Huck and Jim of their dignity, it is because Twain never intended them to be perceived as "a community of saints."[12] The widespread dissatisfaction with the novel's resolution may well spring from the fact that modern readers tend to take Huck and Jim too seriously. If we study them throughout the novel, we will see that they are attractive but imperfect. Recognizing their limitations should prepare us for the conclusion, a conclusion that disappoints only if we insist on believing both characters to be heroic and exempt, somehow, from Twain's often stated belief that all men are fools.

Huck is something of a skeptic, as shown by his disregard for Miss Watson's vision of Providence and his unwillingness to accept "Tom Sawyer's lies" when Tom tries to pretend that a Sunday school picnic is a crowd of Spaniards, Arabs, and elephants. He believes in basing his decisions on what he can see and touch, and this makes him seem shrewder than most of the adults in the novel. But he is also a young boy whose life is frequently shaped by superstition. In the opening chapter of the novel he is horrified when he accidentally kills a spider, convinced that this means that serious bad luck will befall him. He sees nothing comic in Jim's belief in witches. And when a drowned man is pulled from the river, he tells us that he knew "mighty well that a drownded man don't float on his back, but on his face"—from which he concludes that the body must belong to "a woman dressed up in man's clothes."

Similarly, he seems to have little patience with sentimentality, or "sentimentering" as he puts it. When he listens to the king eulogize the conveniently deceased Peter Wilks, he is disgusted by all the "soul-butter and hogwash." He seems here to be wonderfully clear-headed, but he is not always so insightful. He admires Emmeline Grangerford's drawings, for example, and he describes the unspeakably awful "Ode to Stephen Dowling Bots, Dec'd" as "very good poetry." More seriously, he sees nothing ridiculous in the way the Grangerfords indulge in sentimental gestures—like keeping Emmeline's room just the way she had left it—while shooting their neighbors on sight.

Basically honest, Huck nonetheless tells lies throughout the novel, lies which are excusable only because they are absurdly transparent. When he masquerades as a girl and visits St. Petersburg in order to learn the local news, he does such a bad job of it that his disguise is quickly penetrated. He cannot even remember the name he has assumed, a tendency which afflicts him at the Grangerfords as well. After he has forgotten his assumed name, he has to trick Buck Grangerford into revealing it to him, and he then has to write it down so he won't forget it again. When he is interrogated by Joanna Wilks a few chapters later, he lies as cleverly as he can. Nonetheless, he is obliged to admit: "But I didn't do it pretty good, and when I got done I see she warn't satisfied." And when Aunt Sally plies him with questions upon his arrival at the Phelps plantation, he is clearly about to falter. He is not inventive enough to lie with the abandon of a Tom Sawyer, and he confesses, "I was getting so uneasy I couldn't listen good."

On at least one occasion, however, Huck lies very

well indeed. He has been separated from Jim in a fog while scouting about in the canoe. Jim becomes convinced that Huck has drowned and bitterly mourns his loss. When Huck returns to the raft, Jim is asleep; he wakes him up and then pretends that he had never been off the raft: Jim must have dreamed the entire incident. Jim is momentarily taken in, but he eventually realizes that Huck is playing a cruel trick upon him. He rebukes Huck in an often cited scene:

When I got all wore out wid work, en wid de callin' for you, en went to sleep, my heart wuz mos' broke bekase you wuz los', en I didn' k'yer no mo' what become er me en de raf'. En when I wake up en fine you back agin', all safe en soun', de tears come en I could a got down on my knees en kiss' yo' foot I's so thankful. En all you wuz thinkin 'bout wuz how you could make a fool uv ole Jim wid a lie. Dat truck dah is *trash*; en trash is what people is dat puts dirt on de head er dey fren's en makes 'em ashamed.

Huck is mortified, and he tells us, "I could almost kissed *his* foot to get him to take it back." He learns an important lesson: Jim is a man with feelings and not simply a runaway slave upon whom practical jokes can be played at random. "It was fifteen minutes before I could work myself up to go and humble myself to a nigger—but I done it, and I warn't ever sorry for it afterwards, neither. I didn't do him no more mean tricks, and I wouldn't done that one if I'd knowed it would make him feel that way." True to his word, Huck never lies to Jim again, although the stories he tells nearly everyone else reflect his belief that "a body that ups and tells the truth . . . is taking considerable many risks."

As this scene with Jim suggests, Huck is basically kindhearted. Despite a childhood positively drenched with violence, he is deeply troubled by the suffering of others. When he sees house lights burning late at night, he assumes that is "where there was sick folks, may be." When he steals a chicken for his supper, he takes care to choose one "that warn't roosting comfortable." And when he sees a circus performer delighting a crowd by pretending to fall off a horse, he records: "It warn't funny to me, though; I was all of a tremble to see his danger." More seriously, after witnessing the death of Buck Grangerford, he cannot tell us what he saw:

It made me so sick I most fell out of the tree. I ain't agoing to tell *all* that happened—it would make me sick again if I was to do that. I wished I hadn't ever come ashore that night, to see such things. I ain't ever going to get shut of them—lots of times I dream about them.

And he is also haunted by the memory of a slave auction, "the two sons [sold] up the river to Memphis, and their mother down the river to Orleans." Huck recounts "I can't ever get it out of my memory, the sight of them poor miserable girls and niggers hanging around each other's necks and crying."

So great is Huck's capacity to sympathize with suffering that he even has pity for scoundrels. Early in the novel he worries about a gang of thieves trapped on a wrecked steamboat likely to sink at any moment: "I begun to think how dreadful it was, even for murderers, to be in such a fix. I says to myself, there ain't no telling but I might come to be a murderer myself, and then how would *I* like it?" And even after the king and the duke have engineered Jim's capture, Huck cannot bear to see them tarred and feathered:

Well it made me sick to see it; and I was sorry for them poor pitiful rascals, it seemed like I couldn't ever feel any hardness against them any more in the world. It was a dreadful thing to see. Human beings *can* be awful cruel to one another.

But it is important to remember that Huck is still a child, and this helps to account for what otherwise may seem to be contradictions in his character. Despite his genuine horror at the cruelty men and women can inflict on one another, Huck is still capable of rushing "to get a good place at the window" when the fatally wounded Boggs is brought into a Bricksville drug store to die. And he has the child's ability to put trouble behind him. When he realizes that three men have died on the wreck of the *Walter Scott*,[13] he quickly bounces back: "I felt a little bit heavy-hearted about the gang, but not much, for I reckoned if they could stand it, I could." Even more strikingly, within hours of witnessing the gruesome death of Buck Grangerford, he is feasting on pork, cabbage, and buttermilk, feeling "free and safe" on the raft:

I was powerful glad to get away from the feuds, and so was Jim. . . . We said there warn't no home like a raft, after all. Other places do seem so cramped up and smothery, but a raft don't. You feel mighty free and easy and comfortable on a raft.

Huck may be adept at fending for himself, but he lacks confidence in his own judgments—usually because he is the victim of a childlike tendency to see things out of proportion. He regularly defers to Tom Sawyer, for example, because he sees Tom as his superior, foolishly believing that Tom has "style," something which he himself will never attain, "not being brung up to it." More seriously, he sees himself as irredeemably wicked, a view the reader is unlikely to share. When Mary Jane Wilks promises to pray for him, he compares himself to Judas and is amazed by her goodwill: "I reckoned if she'd knowed me she'd take a job that was more nearer her size." Convinced of his own inadequacy, Huck almost always blames himself for anything that goes wrong. He tells us that his conscience "ain't got no sense" and promptly illustrates the point by recording that he felt "to blame, somehow" for the fate that befalls the king and the duke.

It is important to remember these aspects of Huck's character when we examine the struggle through which he passes before deciding to help Jim escape from slavery. Huck sees nothing admirable in his actions; on the contrary, he takes them as a final proof of his own wickedness.

The more I studied about this, the more my conscience went to grinding me, and the more wicked and low-down and onery I got to feeling. And at last, when it hit me all of a sudden that here was the plain hand of Providence slapping me in the face and letting me know my wickedness was being watched all the time from up there in heaven, whilst I was stealing a poor old woman's nigger that hadn't ever done me no harm, and now was showing me there's One that's always on the lookout, and ain't agoing to allow no such miserable doings to go only just so fur and no further, I most dropped in my tracks I was so scared. Well, I tried the best I could to kinder soften it up somehow for myself, by saying I was brung up wicked, and so I warn't so much to blame; but something inside of me kept saying, "There was the Sunday school, you could a gone to it and if you'd a done it, they'd a learnt you, there, that people that acts as I'd been acting about that nigger goes to everlasting fire."

The irony of this passage is that what Huck intends as self-condemnation ultimately emerges as a condemnation of the sort of Christianity that not only tolerated slavery, but actively supported it. We sympathize with Huck and approve of his decision to help Jim regardless of the consequences. But whatever our own feelings toward Huck, we must recognize that his negative conception of himself never abates. As a result, Huck is unable to become an adult. If, at the end of the novel, Huck seems to have come full circle, returning to the sort of boyish "adventures" in which Tom Sawyer specializes, it is because he lacks self-confidence.

When driven into a corner, he almost always does the right thing. But his crucial choices are always made reluctantly, and he never comes to an understanding of their real worth.

In deciding to help Jim, Huck has listened to his heart. But the heart of a fourteen-year-old boy provides an unsteady guide at best. While there can be no question that Huck has chosen rightly, it would be unreasonable to assume that his ability to make this decision means that all his subsequent decisions will be wise and just. Indeed, there is good reason to believe that Huck's resolution will waver, since he had made a similar "decision" earlier in the novel. In chapter 16, Huck records that his "conscience got to stirring up hotter than ever," prompting him to leave the raft intent upon betraying Jim. As Huck paddles away, Jim calls out that he is "de on'y white gentman dat ever kep' his promise to ole Jim." Upon hearing this, Huck reports, "Well I just felt sick." At this point two men come along in another boat and want to search the raft for a runaway slave. Huck has an ideal opportunity to turn Jim in, but he cannot bring himself to do it. Instead he leads the men to think that the raft is infected with smallpox, scaring them away. Realizing that he cannot abandon Jim, Huck returns to the raft "feeling bad and low," because he believes he has failed to do his duty. He thinks the situation over and comes to an interesting conclusion:

Then I thought a minute, and says to myself, hold on,—s'pose you'd a done that right and give Jim up; would you felt better than what you do now? No, says I, I'd feel just the same way I do now. Well, then, says I, what's the use you learning to do right, when it's troublesome to do right, and ain't no trouble to do wrong, and the wages is just the same? I was stuck. I couldn't answer that. So I reckoned I wouldn't bother no more about it, but after this always do whichever come handiest at the time.

It is important to recognize that this is precisely what Huck does *not* do henceforth. His determination to do "whichever come handiest" is short-lived. Fifteen chapters later, he is still trying to make up his mind what to do about Jim. There is no reason to believe that his decision to stand by Jim, even if it means going to hell, will last any longer than his earlier resolution. Huck instinctively knows what is right, but because doing right violates the social norms to which he is accustomed, and because he is still only a child, he is constantly vulnerable to relapse. If his behavior at the end of the novel is inconsistent with his "best self," it should come as no surprise; his ability to live up to his newly acquired code is erratic throughout the book.

Thus, almost immediately after deciding to rescue Jim from the Phelps plantation, Huck is capable of the following exchange with Aunt Sally. He tells her that his steamboat had "blowed out a cylinder-head," and Aunt Sally is alarmed:

> "Good gracious! Anybody hurt?"
> "No'm. Killed a nigger.
> "Well, it's lucky; because sometimes people do get hurt."

There is irony here, but the irony is all Twain's. There is nothing to suggest that Huck is speaking tongue-in-cheek; like Aunt Sally, he does not consider "a nigger" to be "anybody." He has already forgotten the lesson he had learned through living with Jim on the raft. But this is as it should be. Huck is still a child, and forgetting lessons—or remembering them only sporadically—is a common phenomenon among children.

Equally childlike is Huck's inability to believe that Tom Sawyer is willing to help Jim escape. His own determination to help Jim springs from "wickedness"; Tom, on the other hand, is "respectable, and well brung up." Ironically, Huck is right. Tom *is* too respectable to help a slave escape; he does so only as a prank, knowing that Jim is already free. But the irony is in the situation, not in Huck's point of view. Huck is being perfectly straightforward when he writes, "I'm bound to say Tom Sawyer fell, considerable, in my estimation. . . . Tom Sawyer, a *nigger-stealer!*" Whatever insight he has gained during his voyage down the river, he has not completely abandoned the values of the society around him: Tom is still his friend, and Aunt Sally recognizes him as kin. He may dream of escaping to the Territory, but he is destined to return to St. Petersburg.

Critics who insist on viewing *Huckleberry Finn* as a "novel of education" put themselves in a position in which they must reject the conclusion, or justify it through ingenious arguments about structure and form. It would be more accurate to read the book as chronicling an ongoing struggle that is never entirely resolved. The very seriousness of Huck's concerns militates against pat conclusions. Huck is a boy at the beginning of the novel, and he is still a boy at the end—a boy who happens to be a few months older, and a boy who has had experiences from which he may ultimately profit, but still a boy who is in the process of growing up, with all the uncertainty and confusion that implies.

If modern critics have been apt to take Huck too seriously, they have tended to do the same with Jim, celebrating him as a larger-than-life figure. According to Roger Salomon, both Huck and Jim "are related to the demigods of the river, to the barbarous primitivism of the Negro, and beyond that to the archetypal primitives of the Golden Age, instinctively good, uncorrupted by reason, living close to nature and more influenced by its portents than by the conventions of civilization."[14] James Cox is only slightly more moderate. Describing Jim as "the conscience of the novel, the

spiritual yardstick by which all men are measured,"
Cox also turns Jim into a walking myth—the "great res-
idue of primitive, fertile force."[15] So pervasive is this
trend that other critics have even praised Jim for being
superstitious. Walter Blair believes that when Jim
speaks of witches, his "soaring improvisations prove
his mastery of supernatural lore."[16] And Gladys Bellamy sounds almost infatuated, admiring Jim for his
"manly qualities" and the "dark knowledge that lies in
his blood and his nerve ends."[17]

There can be no question that Twain intended his
readers to feel sympathetic toward Jim. The runaway
slave plays a vital role in helping Huck survive. Although it is Huck who discovers the cave on Jackson's
Island, it is Jim who insists that they make their camp
within it, pointing out that it is going to rain. Jim is
proved right; it soon begins to rain "like all fury," and
Huck is delighted to be comfortably settled in the
cave. "Jim, this is nice," he says. "I wouldn't want to be
nowhere else but here." And Jim responds by reminding Huck—and the reader—that he is responsible for
their well being:

Well, you wouldn't a ben here, 'f it hadn't a ben for Jim. You'd
a ben down dah in de woods widout any dinner, en gittin'
mos' drownded, too, dat you would, honey.

In a manner of speaking, Jim has provided a home for
Huck—something he does once again, after they have
left the island for the raft. It is Jim who builds a shelter
on the raft, protecting them from bad weather and the
lapping of the waves. He knows how to do things and
is experienced in the art of survival.

Moreover, his loyalty and kindness are remarkable in a book populated mostly with scoundrels. He
remains faithful to Huck throughout the book—and, at
the end, he is loyal even to Tom Sawyer, a boy who
has done nothing but injure him during the last several

weeks. And the text makes it clear that Jim is deeply attached to his children. Huck tells us:

I went to sleep, and Jim didn't call me when it was my turn. He often done that. When I waked up, just at day-break, he was setting there with his head down betwixt his knees, moaning and mourning to himself. I didn't take notice, nor let on. I knowed what it was about. He was thinking about his wife and his children, away up yonder, and he was low and homesick; because he hadn't ever been away from home before in his life; and I do believe he cared just as much for his people as white folks does for their'n. It does not seem natural, but I reckon it's so. He was often moaning and mourning, that way, nights, when he judged I was asleep, and saying, "Po little 'Lizabeth! po' little Johnny! it's mighty hard; I spec' I ain't ever gwyne to see you no mo'!" He was a mighty good nigger, Jim was.

The carefully controlled understatement of Huck's closing line helps drive the point home. Jim is indeed "mighty good."

Nonetheless, Jim is portrayed as being extraordinarily gullible and something of a comic figure. Back in St. Petersburg, Jim had been a local celebrity by virtue of his account of how witches had put him in a trance and rode him all over the state. Every time Jim tells his story, it becomes increasingly dramatic. The origin of the tale could hardly be more trivial: Jim had wakened one night to find his hat hanging from a tree—where it had been placed by Tom Sawyer as a practical joke. But he seems to believe his own, more colorful version:

Jim was monstrous proud about it, and he got so he wouldn't hardly notice the other niggers. Niggers would come from miles to hear Jim tell about it, and he was more looked up to than any nigger in that country. . . . Niggers is always talking about witches in the dark by the kitchen fire; but whenever one was talking and letting on to know all about such things, Jim would happen in and say, "Hm! What you know 'bout witches?" and that nigger was corked up and had to take a back seat. . . . Jim was most ruined, for a servant, because he got so stuck up on account of having seen the devil and been rode by witches.

Surely there is nothing admirable about believing in witchcraft and turning one's delusions into a source of pride. So far from being some sort of wonderful "dark knowledge" worthy of our respect, Jim's belief in witches makes him look foolish. It also links him to the slave on the Phelps plantation who brings him his meals, a pathetic character, with a "chuckle-headed face, and his wool . . . all tied up in little bunches with thread," who is convinced that witches are always after him. Twain's humor is at Jim's expense.

More seriously, Jim's passive acceptance of his imprisonment on the Phelps plantation, and his foolish toleration of the punishment the boys inflict upon him, are both perfectly consistent with his behavior throughout the novel. He seems to have been exhausted by his one bold action—his flight to Jackson's Island. Thereafter, he drifts down the river, taking orders from a fourteen-year-old boy and willingly dressing up as "a sick Arab" when told to do so. Although he knows how to cook catfish and make corn bread, he is ultimately helpless when it comes to asserting himself and realizing his own escape from bondage. He entrusts himself to Huck, and when they drift past Cairo—all too significantly—he accepts the situation with disappointing ease.

Jim's willingness to go along with the absurdities of Tom Sawyer's grand "evasion" should therefore come as no surprise to critics. Jim has been "going along" throughout most of the book. Had Twain meant Jim to be the hero of the novel, he would have allowed him to escape as the result of his own ingenuity—or at least through Huck's, since Huck is, to an extent, his adopted son. But the ending of *Huckleberry*

Finn makes it clear that Jim's flight down the Mississippi lacked any real meaning. Jim has been free for months—not by virtue of his own action, but by the unexpected generosity of Miss Watson. Here is the ultimate indignity. To picture Jim in the last few scenes of the novel is to picture a man dressed in woman's clothing who is about to discover that he owes his life to the kindness of the mistress he betrayed. But Jim shows no resentment, not even any embarrassment. When Tom Sawyer pays him forty dollars for his trouble, he is absolutely delighted. "I *tole* you I bin rich wunst," he happily proclaims, "en gwineter to be rich *agin*; en it's come true; en heah she *is*!" The modern reader may be forgiven for wishing that Jim had told all those nice white folk to go to hell. Instead, he dances off the stage like a jolly buffoon, the comic Negro from a nineteenth-century minstrel show.

This conclusion would have been inconceivable if Twain had intended the work to celebrate Jim. It is true that Twain was bitterly opposed to slavery. But by the time he wrote *Huckleberry Finn*, he had come to think little of men in general, referring frequently to "the damned human race." Because he considered slavery to be cruel and unjust, it does not follow that he believed the slave superior to the master. Jim has definite limitations. And when Huck bestows upon him his highest praise, saying that he knew Jim was "white inside," it comes as a distinctly mixed blessing in a novel populated with extraordinarily disagreeable whites. Rather than reading *Huckleberry Finn* as a tribute to "the barbarous primitivism of the Negro," and then complaining that Twain wrote a conclusion that betrayed this interpretation, it would be more accurate to see the work as denying any fundamental difference between white and black, by revealing that both are subject to the same follies.

If the analysis of characterization is crucial to understanding *Huckleberry Finn*, it does not reveal what it is about the novel that makes it so compelling. Both Huck and Jim are engaging and memorable characters, but their story is ultimately a vehicle that enabled Twain to explore broader concerns.

For many years it was customary to see the novel focused upon a contrast between the river and the shore as metaphors, respectively, for freedom and slavery—to see the journey down the river as an escape from the bondage of modern civilization. This reading springs from the American illusion that "freedom" can be found through movement and constant change of locale. When Huck confesses, "All I wanted was to go somewheres; all I wanted was a change, I warn't particular," he voices a profoundly American desire. But readers who believe that Huck finds happiness on the river, and that his projected flight to the Territory will free him from the anxieties that have afflicted him throughout the book, are victims of precisely the sort of romantic self-deception the work is aimed against. The river takes Huck from the Widow Douglas, but it delivers him to Aunt Sally Phelps. One of the most disturbing aspects of *Huckleberry Finn* is the way in which it consistently rejects the possibility of escape.

Consider Huck's description of life on the raft at its most idyllic:

It was kind of solemn, drifting down the big still river, laying on our backs looking up at the stars, and we didn't ever feel like talking loud, and it warn't often that we laughed, only a little kind of low chuckle. We had mighty good weather, as a general thing, and nothing ever happened to us at all, that night, nor the next, nor the next.

This passage is often cited to illustrate the freedom of life on the Mississippi. But such tranquil moments are intermittent at best. Huck himself seems surprised to be able to report that "nothing ever happened to us" for three nights in a row. They are usually under siege— by bounty hunters, steamboat pilots, treacherous currents, and dangerous fogs. As the river carries the powerless raft into the Deep South, it exposes both Huck and Jim to numerous threats. It can offer no real protection from the men who travel upon it.

Moreover, the river is destructive in its own right, as shown by the description of a town built on its shore:

On the river front some of the houses was sticking out over the bank, and they was bowed and bent, and about ready to tumble in. . . . The bank was caved away under one corner of some others, and that corner was hanging over. People lived in them yet, but it was dangersome, because sometimes a strip of land as wide as a house caves in at a time. Sometimes a belt of land a quarter of a mile deep will start in and cave along and cave along till it all caves into the river in one summer. Such a town as that has to be always moving back, and back, and back, because the river's always gnawing at it.

On one level, this passage is an indictment of the people who inhabit the town. Only a degenerate civilization would continue to live in houses that are about to tumble into a river. On the other hand, the river seems to be to blame for the state of these people's lives. It is the river, after all, that forces them "back, and back, and back"—a phrase that suggests the town is moving "backward" in more sense than one. As the river is "always gnawing" at the town, the town continues to decline, and as the town declines, its inhabitants become increasingly primitive. The river does not represent "freedom" so much as anarchy.

Huck is drawn into the town in question here because, by this point in the novel, he has lost control of the raft. From the moment the king and the duke board the raft, serenity is a thing of the past. Jim quite

rightly dislikes the two imposters as "regular rapscallions." But he and Huck nonetheless find themselves
reduced to being servants on the raft that had briefly
been their own domain. Throughout most of their
journey, Huck and Jim are thus doubly helpless, their
direction determined by the current of the river, their
schedule fixed by their passengers. The significance of
this dilemma should not be underestimated. The boy
and the slave both flee to the river in order to escape
from restraint and are driven onward by the illusion
that they can control their own destinies. But what follows serves only to illustrate the futility of this attempt.
They can master neither the raft nor the river and, as a
result, find themselves increasingly helpless as the
novel moves along.

Arguing that the novel reflects "a vision of life's
absurdity," David Burg has pointed out that Huck and
Jim "cannot change the order of things; all they can do
is endure."[18] They are helpless, on an immediate level,
because they have limited knowledge and experience.
But the novel as a whole is permeated with such a deep
sense of melancholy that it is impossible not to feel that
all men are doomed to similar failure. No matter what
one's skills at navigation, one must still have a destination for which to sail. Having encouraged us to sympathize with both Huck and Jim, Twain forces us to ask
where they could possibly go—and, by extension,
where could we go if we wanted to be free. There can
be no satisfying answer to this question once it has
been raised. But Twain deserves credit for refusing to
provide an easy answer. If readers are often disappointed with the conclusion of *Huckleberry Finn*, it
may be because they crave the sort of "happy ending"
Twain could not in honesty provide. In the process of
rejecting nineteenth-century romanticism, he had come
to a distinctly modern point of view—the idea that,
whatever the shortcomings of the world in which we

live, it is nevertheless a world from which there is no exit.

One of the reasons why Huck inspires so much sympathy is that he is painfully isolated within this world. The ultimate loner, he is condemned to wander but never to belong. The most consistent aspect of his character may be his loneliness. While still living with the Widow Douglas, he tells us that "I felt so lonesome I most wished I was dead," and he finds the house at night to be "as still as death." After he has made camp on Jackson's Island, he admits that "by-and-by it got sort of lonesome," and his response is to go to sleep, observing "there ain't no better way to put in time when you are lonesome." Practically the first thing he records after discovering Jim is "I warn't lonesome now." But he is frequently separated from Jim in the chapters that follow, finding it "dismal and lonesome." By the time he goes to rescue Jim from the Phelps plantation, Huck's loneliness seems to have developed into melancholia. Consider the way he responds to a sunny summer day:

When I got there it was all still and Sunday-like, and hot and sunshiny—the hands was gone to the fields; and there was them kind of faint dronings of bugs and flies in the air that makes it seem so lonesome and like everybody's dead and gone; and if a breeze fans along and quivers the leaves, it makes you feel mournful, because you feel like it's spirits whispering—spirits that's been dead ever so many years— and you always think they're talking about *you*. As a general thing it makes a body wish *he* was dead, too, and done with it all.

Shortly afterward, he hears a spinning wheel, and his response is to focus on its "wailing," confessing that "then I knowed for certain I wished I was dead—for that *is* the lonesomest sound in the world." Such feelings as these are more likely to afflict a man approaching fifty than a boy in the flush of early adolescence, and it may be that Twain is speaking through Huck. But we must nevertheless recognize that whatever his occasional high spirits, Huck is anxious and depressed throughout much of the book.

Huck's sense of isolation is heightened by the fact that he is haunted by death. He feigns his own death, discovers a dead man in the river, sees Buck Granger-ford killed in the climax of a dreadful feud, and watches horrified as Col. Sherburn shoots a drunken old man in the middle of a public street. A few chapters later, when he is desperate to hide some gold from the king and the duke, Huck is drawn to the coffin bearing the remains of Peter Wilks, where he tucks the money "down below where his hands was crossed, which made me creep they was so cold." He subsequently attends a funeral presided over by a snakelike undertaker—"the softest, glidingest, stealthiest man I ever see"—and, after dark, he is dragged to a graveyard to watch an exhumation. Moreover, the autobiographies that Huck invents are consistently grim, characterized, as they are, by infant brothers who have drowned in the river and fathers who are either dead, or dying of smallpox.[19]

Of all these incidents, the Sherburn episode is the most disquieting. It is completely lacking in humor and climaxes in one of the angriest passages Twain had yet to write. The people of the town have rushed to Sherburn's house, intending to lynch him for shooting an unarmed man. But Sherburn is not intimidated; he denounces the crowd in a speech that is worth quoting at length:

"The idea of *you* lynching anybody! It's amusing. The idea of you thinking you had pluck enough to lynch a *man*! Because you're brave enough to tar and feather poor friendless cast-out women that come along here, did that make you think you had grit enough to lay your hands on a *man*? Why, a *man's* safe in the hands of ten thousand of your kind—as long as it's day-time and you're not behind him.

"Do I know you? I know you clear through. I was born and raised in the South, and I've lived in the North; so I know the average all around. The average man's a coward. . . . Why don't your juries hang murderers? Because they're afraid the man's friends will shoot them in the back, in the dark—and it's just what they *would* do. . . .

"You didn't want to come. The average man don't like trouble and danger. *You* don't like trouble and danger. . . . The pitifulest thing out is a mob; that's what an army is—a mob; they don't fight with courage that's born in them, but with courage that's borrowed from their mass, and from their officers. But a mob without any *man* at the head of it, is *beneath* pitifulness. Now the thing for *you* to do, is to droop your tails and go home and crawl in a hole. If any real lynching's going to be done, it will be done in the dark, Southern fashion; and when they come they'll bring their masks and fetch a *man* along. Now *leave*. . . ."

Technically speaking, this passage is a flaw in the narration of the novel; it is the only passage of any length that is presented to us as if direct from a secondary character with no trace of Huck's own inflection. It is difficult to believe that Huck could have remembered such a long speech so thoroughly as to be able to present it verbatim. It would have been more natural for him to simply summarize the speech in his own words. Most critics agree that Sherburn's denunciation of "the average man" reflects Twain's own point of view, and it cannot be denied that the voice in question here will be heard with increasing frequency in the works that follow *Huckleberry Finn*. But to dwell on this point is to overlook the significance of what Sherburn has said and how it relates thematically to the novel in which it appears. Sherburn's speech serves, within *Huckleberry Finn*, to accentuate the alienation from society from which Huck himself suffers. Sherburn lacks Huck's compassion, but he is the man Huck might become. If

Huck never stands before a crowd and tells them to go to hell, it is because he is, as yet, too weak and vulnerable to do so. But like Sherburn, Huck has a low opinion of most men, having observed at close range the selfishness that inspires most action. It is significant that when he wishes to keep some men from searching the raft on which Jim is hiding, Huck decides to beg for their help, implying that his father is ill with smallpox. As we know, the ruse works; the men are scared away, illustrating Sherburn's belief that "the average man's a coward," a belief that Huck apparently shares. Huck has already seen enough of life to know that "Human beings *can* be awful cruel to one another," and we have seen how he is moved, at one point, to feel "ashamed of the human race." Thus, whatever their difference in diction and degree, the distance between Huck and Sherburn is not so great as it may seem. They are both alienated from the society in which they are forced to live.

It should be clear, therefore, that however idyllic *The Adventures of Huckleberry Finn* may seem when cast in the glow of a Mississippi sunset, it has a distinctly somber side that anticipates some of the central concerns of modern fiction. Hemingway believed that "All modern American literature comes from one book by Mark Twain called *Huckleberry Finn*,"[20] which is, of course, an exaggeration. But if *Huck* continues to be read more frequently than any other American novel, it is because it speaks so eloquently of dilemmas that continue to confront us. Although children are apt to dwell upon Huck's rebellious escapades, the sophisticated reader is almost certain to be struck by what a sad and moving work this is.

5

vvvvvvvvvvvvvvvvvvvvvvvvvvvvvvvvvvvvvvvvvvvvvvv

Invincible Stupidity:
A Connecticut Yankee in King Arthur's Court

Written between 1884 and 1889, *A Connecticut Yankee in King Arthur's Court* is one of Mark Twain's most controversial works. Twain wrote that "the story isn't a satire peculiarly, it is more especially a *contrast*."[1] But critics are sharply divided when it comes to deciding the meaning of this contrast between the sixth century and the nineteenth. Twain's contemporaries received the book as a celebration of modern values—William Dean Howells describing it as "an object lesson in democracy."[2] More recently, Henry Nash Smith has argued that *A Connecticut Yankee* "precipitated in Mark Twain something like a negative conversion, a loss of faith in progress and human perfection."[3] And another critic has gone even further in rejecting the idea that the novel idealizes nineteenth-century civilization. Whatever its "official theme," Roger B. Salomon finds its real theme to be "the absurdity of optimism and the impermanence of progress . . . because of the aggressiveness and rapacity of modern industrial man, the false promise of technology and—ultimately—because of the deep-rootedness of human evil."[4] The fundamental question concerning *A Connecticut Yankee in King Arthur's Court* is then one that determines the way in which we should read this book: Does it advance the blessings of technology or attack those who put their faith in machines? Clearly, this is a work that deserves to be read closely.

Twain prefaced *A Connecticut Yankee* with "A Word of Explanation" designed to account for the tale that he is about to unfold. He tells us that, while touring Warwick Castle, he met a "curious stranger" who later gave to him a manuscript "yellow with age." We learn that the stranger's name is Hank Morgan, and the forty-four chapters that follow are presented as if they came directly from the manuscript he left with Twain.

The superintendent of a great arms factory in nineteenth-century Connecticut, Hank is hit over the head with a crowbar during a quarrel with one of the men under him. When he comes to, he finds himself transported back to sixth-century England, on the outskirts of Camelot. At first he thinks that he has stumbled into a lunatic asylum, but it gradually dawns on him that he may indeed have been magically transported into the past. He quickly determines upon a course of action, telling us, "if it was still the nineteenth century and I was among lunatics and couldn't get away, I would presently boss that asylum or know the reason why; and if on the other hand it was really the sixth century . . . I would boss the whole country inside of three months; for I judged I would have the start of the best-educated man in the kingdom by a matter of thirteen hundred years and upwards."

Captured by one of the knights of the Round Table, Morgan is condemned as a "man-devouring ogre" and sentenced to be burned at the stake. But thanks to an encyclopedic knowledge uncharacteristic of factory foremen, Hank recalls that an eclipse of the sun is close at hand. He proclaims himself a magician and announces that he will blot out the sun forevermore if he is harmed. Just as he is being chained to the stake, the eclipse conveniently begins, and the court is duly terrified. The king entreats Morgan to restore the sun, and Hank agrees on condition that the king appoint him "perpetual minister and executive" entitled to "one per cent of such actual increase of revenue over and above its present amount" that he expects to create for the state. The king agrees to these terms; the eclipse comes to a timely end, and Morgan becomes "The Boss"—second in power only to King Arthur.

Determined to "civilize" Camelot by introducing modern industrial technology, Morgan establishes various factories in the countryside, allowing no one near them except by special permit. He fears the power of the Church and believes that he may be overthrown if he brings about change too quickly: "The people could not have stood it; and moreover I should have had the Established Roman Catholic Church on my back in a minute." For the next four years, he prepares "the nuclei of future vast factories, the iron and steel missionaries of my future civilization," but he does so in secret, consolidating his position as a great magician.

Because he finds it politically expedient to seem as if he shares the values of the people around him, Morgan eventually is forced to leave the court on a knightly quest. He travels into the country with the Demoiselle Alisande la Carteloise—whom he promptly nicknames "Sandy"—in order to liberate forty-five "princesses" held captive in "a castle" by "three ogres."

In one of the less successful scenes of the novel, Twain satirizes the medieval tendency to romanticize by revealing the castle to be a pigsty, the princesses hogs, and the ogres swineherds. But having sent his Yankee into the English countryside, Twain is able to provide him with numerous adventures along the way. Hank visits the dungeons of Morgan Le Fay, restores a reputedly miraculous fountain, and—most importantly—meets a variety of men and women who would never have appeared at court, thus enabling Twain to broaden his presentation of sixth-century life.

This device is familiar to us from Twain's earlier works. Chapters are organized like those of a travel-

ogue, devoted, in this case, to an innocent abroad in
the sixth century. This is a convenient device in that it
allows Twain to treat chapters as separate units, each
devoted to chronicling a particular adventure, but only
loosely organized in terms of logical sequence. And
when Hank's journey with Sandy comes to an end,
Twain characteristically sends him off on another, this
time with King Arthur. Traveling incognito, the two
most powerful men in Britain set out to explore the nature of the kingdom over which they rule.

The chapters that are devoted to this second journey emphasize the harshness of life in medieval Britain.
Our pilgrims see a woman stoned "until she hardly
looked human," and they watch as another is executed
for stealing a small piece of cloth she had hoped to sell
in order to feed her starving child. Their journey ends
when they find themselves seized and sold into slavery.
Hank manages to escape, but he is soon recaptured
and condemned to death with the other slaves. Arthur
tries to explain that he is the king, but no one recognizes him since he is in rags. It looks as if both the king
and the Boss are about to die, but they are rescued, at
the last moment, by five hundred knights—called to
the scene by a message Hank had been secretly able to
dispatch.

Safely back in Camelot, Hank decides that the
time has now come to impose upon Britain the technology he has been nurturing over the years. He determines "to destroy knight-errantry or be its victim"
(which hardly seems generous of him, since he now
owes his life to the fidelity of the same knights he has
vowed to destroy). He enters a tournament and shoots
his knightly foe dead with a revolver. He thereupon
dares "the chivalry of England to come against [him]—
not by individuals, but in mass!" Hundred of knights
promptly accept this challenge, but they break ranks
and flee after Hank quickly shoots nine more men

dead. Since this is many centuries before firearms were known in Europe, it looks as if Hank has triumphed through black magic.

Believing that he has "broke the back of knight-errantry," Hank exposes his hidden schools and factories to public view, establishes railroads and telephones, sets steamboats running on the Thames, and converts the Round Table into a stock board. For three full years, medieval England seems to flourish, thanks to the benefits of modern technology.

Hank and Sandy have married by now and produced a daughter. When the child falls ill, doctors urge that she be taken to the French coast to recover. And while Hank is abroad, his new civilization crumbles. A civil war erupts, and the Church imposes an interdict. Upon his return to England, Hank finds that all of England is marching against him—all but fifty-two boys, who were the product of his special schools, and his chief lieutenant Clarence.

Hank leads this small band to a fortified cave. Protected by an electrified fence and armed with torpedoes and machine guns, Hank prepares to fight. When the enemy approaches, he throws a switch and electrifies some eleven thousand men. His machine guns "vomit death" into the ranks of those who make it past the fence, and within minutes "armed resistance was totally annihilated, the campaign was ended. . . . Twenty-five thousand men lay dead around us."

After the battle is over, Hank leaves his fortress in order to aid the wounded. As he bends over a crippled knight, he is stabbed by the man he sought to help. His comrades bring him back to the cave, where they soon realize that they are trapped. They can defend themselves only from their cave, and it is surrounded by the putrefying flesh of twenty-five thousand corpses. Gradually they all fall ill. Then Merlin makes his way into the cave, where he casts a spell over Hank Morgan so that he will sleep for thirteen centuries, enabling Hank to meet Mark Twain in late nineteenth-century England.

Our reading of this tale is to a large extent dependent upon how we feel about Hank Morgan. Is he "a good and trustworthy narrator . . . who usually carries the burden of authorial attitudes,"[5] or is he the imaginary forerunner of a modern fascist dictator, leading his people to genocide from the confines of a sixth-century *fuehrer-bunker*?[6]

One of the best descriptions of Hank Morgan is that which he himself provides:

I am an American. I was born and reared in Hartford, in the State of Connecticut—anyway, just over the river, in the country. So I am a Yankee of the Yankees—and practical; yes, and nearly barren of sentiment, I suppose—or poetry, in other words. My father was a blacksmith, my uncle was a horse doctor, and I was both, along at first. Then I went over to the great arms factory and learned my real trade; learned to make everthing; guns, revolvers, cannon, boilers, engines, all sorts of labor-saving machinery. Why I could make anything a body wanted—anything in the world. . . .

It is significant that Hank defines "anything a body wanted" in terms of weapons, the manufacture of which he calls his "real trade." He is associated, therefore, with violence from the moment he first opens his mouth. And it is also worth noting that he sees himself as "barren of sentiment"; those critics who cast him as a humanitarian would do well to bear this in mind.

Twain disassociates himself from Hank by emphasizing his limitations. Consider, for example, the scene in which Morgan first confronts his new world:

It was a soft, reposeful summer landscape, as lovely as a dream, and as lonesome as Sunday. The air was full of the smell of flowers, and the buzzing of insects, and the twittering of birds, and there were no people, no wagons, there was no stir of life, nothing going on.[7]

Set within an idyllic countryside, Hank sees no value in anything about him. The land about him is undeveloped; it would appeal to him only if filled with the signs of industry and commerce. Here is a man who can gaze upon the fruited plain and envision an asphalt parking lot.

Hank's inability to appreciate beauty is revealed even more clearly when, after establishing himself as the second most powerful man in Britain, he finds himself installed in "the choicest suite of apartments in the castle, after the king's." Like a tourist who goes abroad and complains about the plumbing, Hank is dismayed that Camelot is so little like East Hartford. He compares a tapestry to a bed quilt and complains that the walls are decorated only with silken hangings, whereas back home "you couldn't go into a room but you would find an insurance chromo, or at least a three-color God-Bless-Our Home over the door; and in the parlor we had nine."

It could easily be argued that Twain himself placed little value on aesthetics, and that when Hank declares "Raphael was a bird," he is only continuing the attack upon the "old Masters" that Twain had launched in *The Innocents Abroad*. But there is a more serious flaw within Hank's character, one that is impossible to rationalize. Hank consistently reveals himself to be contemptuous of anyone who does not completely share his own point of view.

When he first approaches Camelot, Morgan observes that the men "look like animals," and he later decides that they are "white Indians." He scorns the populace as a whole as "nothing but rabbits," and while he occasionally condescends to see the people as "a childlike and innocent lot," he cannot take them seriously. Because their culture is completely unlike his own, because it is so "unAmerican," it therefore follows that the country is not civilized. Hank tells us:

I saw that I was just another Robinson Crusoe cast away on an uninhabited island, with no society but some more or less tame animals, and if I wanted to make life bearable I must do as he did—invent, contrive, create, reorganize things; set brain and hand to work, and keep them busy.

In short, Hank is incapable of understanding values that are alien to his own; a supreme egotist, he sets out to remake the world in his own image.

As a nineteenth-century entrepreneur, Morgan is the representative within the novel of a seemingly more advanced society. But it soon becomes clear that Hank values nothing so much as making money, and his schemes for doing so reveal a distinctly unattractive side of his character. He boasts that, as a boy, he always substituted buttons for coins when asked to contribute to foreign missions: "The buttons would answer the ignorant savage as well as the coin, the coin would answer me better than the buttons." Now that he finds himself surrounded by men and women who are, in his view, "merely modified savages," Hank grants himself a license to exploit.

Speaking of funerals, he remarks: "the money's in the details; the more details, the more swag: bearers, mutes, candles, prayers—everything counts; and if the bereaved don't buy prayers enough you mark up your candles with a forked pencil, and your bill shows up all right."[8] One scene in particular emphasizes Hank's delight in profiteering. En route to restore a holy fountain—a task that leads him to reflect, "I wished I could charge admission"—Hank encounters Saint Simon Stylite, standing upon a pillar and praying through the peculiar method of "bowing his body ceaselessly and rapidly almost to his feet." Morgan decides that it is "a

pity to have all this power going to waste," so he devises a system of elastic cords through which the sup-
plicant is harnessed to a sewing machine. If the scene
had ended here, the humor would have been at the expense of the saint. But Hank goes on to boast:

I . . . got five years' good service out of him; in which time
he turned out upwards of eighteen thousand first-rate tow-
linen shirts, which was ten a day. I worked him Sundays and
all; he was going Sundays the same as weekdays, and it was
no use to waste the power. These shirts cost me nothing but
just the mere trifle for the materials . . . and they sold like
smoke to pilgrims at a dollar and a half apiece, which was
the price of fifty cows. . . . They were regarded as a perfect
protection against sin, and advertised as such by my knights
everywhere, with the paintpot and stencil plate; insomuch
that there was not a cliff or a boulder or a dead wall in England but you could read on it at a mile distance:
    "Buy the only genuine St. Stylite; patronized by the No-
bility. Patent applied for."

It is characteristic of Hank to regard prayer as a waste
of energy, and his response is to reduce a man to the
level of a machine. There can be no question but that
we are meant to pull away from Hank at this point.
Twain emphasizes the Yankee's greed by describing
how the shirts were sold at an outrageous markup
thanks to false advertising, advertising that desecrated
the natural beauty of the land, as Hank applied "the
paintpot and the stencil plate" to every cliff and
boulder in England. And it is striking that for all his
complaints about the gullibility of the English people,
Hank is willing to exploit their innocence when it
comes to making a profit. He claims that his mission is
to educate and enlighten—and, at times, it is—but he
never allows his liberal principles to interfere with
business.

    Hank's language consistently reveals his true
values. His is the diction of the marketplace. He tells

us, for example, that "It is no use to throw away a good thing merely because the market isn't ripe yet." After he has destroyed Merlin's Tower, he declares that "the account was square, the books balanced." When another of his schemes fails to work out, he tells us that he "sold it short." He mocks the knights because they all "took a flier at the Holy Grail now and then," observing:

There was worlds of reputation in it, but no money. Why, they actually wanted *me* to put in! Well, I should smile.

After all, Hank is much too "practical" to waste time on anything that is not financially remunerative. It should not come then as any surprise that Hank wishes he could remake man without a conscience because conscience "cannot be said to pay."[9]

Ironically, when Hank is enslaved, he criticizes his master for having a heart "solely for business." Weakened by the cold, they encounter a woman who is about to be burned at the stake.

Well, now, what do you suppose our master did? . . . our brute, with a heart solely for business, lashed us into position about the stake and warmed us into life and commercial value by the same fire which took away the innocent life of the poor harmless mother. That was the sort of master we had.

Hank is completely unaware that the slavemaster is only a cruder version of himself; both see men in terms of their commercial value, and neither is apt to allow sentiment to interfere with business. That Twain himself saw a parallel between slavemasters and financiers is established by an illustration in the first edition of *A Connecticut Yankee,* an illustration that Twain singled out for praise: The slavemaster was given the features of Jay Gould, the great robber baron. And it is worth noting, at this point, that Hank is tied by his name to a capitalist of dubious reputation, the great American banker, J. P. Morgan.

It should be evident by now that the characterization of Hank Morgan is not without inconsistencies. The practical superintendent of an arms factory, he has nonetheless read Defoe and seen the Raphael cartoons at Hampton Court. As the book develops, these inconsistencies become more marked. On occasion, Twain uses the Yankee to condemn cruelty and injustice; on other occasions, however, he is the object of Twain's scorn—the modern con-man who is out to enrich himself at any cost. As a result, the novel has been criticized for "an element of obscurity in the narrative that puzzles the modern reader."[10] But it is important to realize that inconsistency is very human; a character may be contradictory but real nonetheless. What appear to be contradictions in Hank's character "are, in fact, a necessary consequence of the Yankee's mental processes, and thus an integral part of his character."[11]

It is easier to understand Hank Morgan when we realize that he is a sentimentalist; he indulges in flights of feeling that seldom ring true. Consider, for example, the following passage, in which Hank recalls the sweetheart he left behind in Connecticut:

Fifteen! Break—my heart! Oh, my lost darling! Just her age who was so gentle, and lovely, and all the world to me, and whom I shall never see again! How the thought of her carries me back over wide seas of memory to a vague dim time, a happy time, so many, many centuries hence, when I used to wake in the soft summer mornings, out of sweet dreams of her, and say "Hello, Central!" just to hear her dear voice come melting back to me with a "Hello, Hank!" that was music of the spheres to my enchanted ear. She got three dollars a week, but she was worth it.

A tribute to a telephone operator named Puss Flanagan, this passage is compounded of a whole series of clichés, only to reveal, in the last line, where Hank's real values lie. The sudden descent from greeting-card sentimentality seems deliberately calculated to make us laugh, and our laughter is directed against Hank. The highest and most original praise he can bestow upon his love is to declare that she earned her keep. But at least this praise has the merit of being sincere. The lines that precede it positively drip with false emotion.

Elsewhere we find Hank indulging in false modesty. Although he is prepared to kill anyone who gets in his way, Morgan objects to the language he hears spoken at Arthur's court. He tells us that it "would have made a Comanche blush. Indelicacy is too mild a term for it." When he is stripped of his clothes, he is amazed that no one attaches much importance to seeing a naked man: "In half a minute I was as naked as a pair of tongs! And dear, dear, to think of it: I was the only embarrassed person there."

Later, when he is obliged to escort Sandy on her quest, he is shocked that there will be no chaperone: "What? She browse around the hills and scour the woods with me—alone—and I as good as engaged to be married? Why it's scandalous. Think how it would look." And during the course of that quest, he sleeps in his armor—even though he is fully clothed underneath—as taking it off "would have seemed so like undressing before folk."

In this respect, Hank Morgan can be seen as the comic embodiment of those characteristics that were considered virtues by the American middle class one hundred years ago. But his modesty, like his capacity for feeling, is only superficial. It is "sentimental" in that it is unreal. But this would be a matter of mild humor were it not for the way in which Hank's sentimentality also colors his politics. He pretends to be a democrat, but his "celebrations of the people are, in fact, extraordinarily superficial; they are nothing more than the patriotic rhetoric his culture has imposed upon him."[12]

However human he likes to see himself, Hank can be cruel when it suits his purposes. Early in the novel, he is shocked to find Morgan Le Fay about to execute a musician for playing poorly. He intervenes in order to avoid "wanton extremities," but after he has heard a performance, he gives permission to hang the entire band. And when he is repairing the Holy Fountain, he initially plans to have "a person of no especial value" drop dynamite into the well in order to blast out the obstruction—completely unconcerned that this plan will cause the death of whoever drops the bomb. It is possible to rationalize this sort of violence as "comic hyperbole," no more serious than the violence of a Roadrunner cartoon. A recent critic has argued that "Twain was working confidently in the comic world of frontier humor where overstatement about death and destruction was a standard mode of evoking laughter."[13] But as the book moves along, it becomes increasingly difficult to see Hank's predilection for violence as nothing more than a form of burlesque.

Consider, for example, the scene in which Hank throws a bomb into a group of knights who are about to attack him. This could be justified as self-defense were it not for the awful satisfaction with which Hank contemplates the result of his handiwork:

Yes, it was a neat thing, very neat and pretty to see. It resembled a steamboat explosion on the Mississippi; and during the next fifteen minutes we stood under a steady drizzle of microscopic fragments of knights and hardware and horseflesh.

This side of Hank's character leads directly to the Battle of the Sand Belt, "one of the most distressing passages in American literature."[14] Thanks to modern technology, Hank is able to electrocute thousands of men by simply throwing a switch. And like an overgrown Tom Sawyer, he surveys the carnage with something alarmingly close to pride. "Land, what a sight!" he exclaims. "We were enclosed in three walls of dead men!"

Hank's ability to kill springs from his lack of real feeling. He does not see men as men but as "human muck," the mass destruction of which is a matter of little concern. Even at best, men are simply automata that can be sent on command to a "Man-Factory" or a "Teacher-Factory." He believes that an ideal citizenry can be programmed by the state.

Training—training is everything; training is all there is *to* a person. We speak of nature; it is folly; there is no such thing as nature; what we call by that misleading name is merely heredity and training. We have no thoughts of our own; no opinions of our own; they are transmitted to us, trained into us. All that is original in us, and therefore fairly credible or discredible to us, can be covered up and hidden by the point of a cambric needle, all the rest being atoms contributed by, and inherited from, a procession of ancestors that stretches back a billion years to the Adam-clan or grasshopper or monkey from whom our race has been so tediously and ostentatiously and unprofitably developed.

It is impossible to miss the scorn in this passage. Hank is basically contemptuous of his fellow man, and if he is occasionally moved to tears by the sight of human suffering, it is only in isolated scenes, all of which involve "a melodramatic family situation—the favorite object of Victorian sentimentality."[15]

Hank's belief that "training is everything" leads him frequently to reflect upon the nature of "inherited ideas." In his view, "Old habit of mind is one of the toughest things to get away from in the world." And this observation provokes an uncharacteristic moment of self-knowledge. Speaking of the frequently unexamined ideas one automatically assumes as a result of the time and place in which one lives, Hank admits: "I had mine, the king and his people theirs." In other words, Hank is as much the victim of his own background as the men and women of Camelot are of theirs.

Nonetheless, Hank never doubts that his "inherited ideas" are superior to those he encounters in sixth-century Britain. With his inordinate belief in training—so suggestive of the modern illusion that problems can always be solved through "education"—Hank easily comes to see himself as representing a master race. Because he is better trained than the people about him—because he knows how to *do* more—Hank sets himself apart from everyone around him. He may declare that "A man *is* a man at bottom" and agree that "men were about all alike, and one man as good as another barring clothes," but he does not really believe that such pronouncements apply to himself. The scene in which Hank restores the Holy Fountain makes it clear that he sees himself as a "superior being":

When I started to the chapel, the populace uncovered and fell back reverently to make a wide way for me, as if I had been some kind of superior being—and I was. I was aware of that. . . . I could hardly get to sleep for glorying over it.

Recognizing this aspect of Hank's character, we should hesitate before accepting his judgments as our own. If Hank scorns the people of sixth-century England, it does not necessarily mean that he is right to do so. As Judith Fetterley has observed, "Behind much of Hank's contempt lies the conviction that he can do what others do far better than they can. His contempt is an inverse expression of his own egotism."[16]

In order to preserve his special status, Hank spends much of his time staging elaborate performances deliberately designed to impress people with his power. He loves, in particular, to terrify. After exploiting the eclipse of the sun, for example, he complacently reflects:

I was in one of the most grand attitudes I ever struck. . . . It was a noble effect. You could *see* the shudder sweep the mass like a wave.

His devotion to the theatrical ultimately leads to his undoing. After he is enslaved, he insists upon engineering an escape that is unnecessarily elaborate. And he admits it:

> One could invent quicker ways, and fully as sure ones, but none that would be as picturesque as this; none that would be made so dramatic.

Eventually he comes to realize that this is a weakness on his part:

> There were plenty of ways to get rid of that officer by some simple and plausible device, but no, I must pick out a picturesque one; it is the crying defect in my character.

But self-knowledge does not lead to any lasting change of heart. Only a few pages later, Hank is rejoicing in the spectacle of five hundred knights riding to his rescue on bicycles. "I was immensely satisfied," he tells us. "Take the whole situation all around, it was one of the gaudiest effects I ever instigated." This aspect of Hank's character leads directly to the Battle of the Sand Belt. When he throws the switch that electrocutes thousands, it is his ultimate special effect. In his words: "*There* was a groan you could *hear*!"

Throughout all of these scenes, Hank has been working against what is, ostensibly, his purpose. He tells us again and again that he wants to educate the people of Arthurian Britain and free them from superstition. But the stunts he devises to enhance his prestige all depend upon exploiting the public's gullibility. He deliberately encourages people to think that he is a magician, keeping his knowledge of technology to himself and a few chosen followers. Hank's professed mission to enlighten the Dark Ages is thus as false as his capacity for feeling, his modesty, and his egalitarian principles. He is, in short, a hypocrite—a hypocrite who is magnificently unaware of the discrepancy between what he asserts and what he believes.

With this understanding of Hank Morgan in mind, it should now be possible to examine the role of the

Church. Opposed by the Church, Hank never misses an opportunity to counterattack, casting it as sinister and oppressive. Because of these frequent denunciations of the Church, it is customary to read *A Connecticut Yankee* as anticlerical. In the words of one important critic, "The villain of the book is clearly the Church."[17] But it should be clear by now that Hank's views are not synonymous with Twain's. Although Hank describes the Church as "an established crime, an established slave pen" that "means death to human liberty and paralysis to human thought," he may be the victim of his own prejudices.

Hank blames "the awful power" of the Roman Catholic Church for all social ills:

In two or three little centuries it had converted a nation of men to a nation of worms. Before the day of the Church's supremacy in the world, men were men, and held their heads up, and had a man's pride and spirit and independence. . . . But then the Church came to the front, with an ax to grind; and she . . . invented "divine rights of kings," and propped it all around, brick by brick, with the Beatitudes . . . she preached (to the commoner) humility, obedience to superiors, the beauty of self-sacrifice; she preached (to the commoner) meekness under insult; preached (still to the commoner, always to the commoner) patience, meanness of spirit, nonresistance under oppression; and she introduced heritable ranks and aristocracies, and taught all the Christian populations of the earth to bow down and worship them.

This view is extreme to say the least. It is also historically inaccurate. There is no evidence to support his claim that the Church "invented" inheritable ranks and aristocracies. Republican government was rare in the ancient world, and most pre-Christian societies were structured in terms of recognized hierarchies in which status was often determined by birth. But it should not be necessary to refute Hank's position by going outside of the book. Twain himself provides ample evidence suggesting that Morgan's condemnation of the Church is unfair.

Fairly early in the novel, Hank is annoyed when a priest exposes the cruelty of a government official:

Something of this disagreeable sort was turning up every now and then. I mean episodes that showed that not all priests were frauds and self-seekers, but that many, even the great majority, of these that were down on the ground among the common people, were sincere and right-hearted, and devoted to the alleviation of human troubles and sufferings. Well, it was a thing which could not be helped, so I seldom fretted about it, and never many minutes at a time. . . . But I did not like it, for it was just the sort of thing to keep people reconciled to an Established Church.

It is characteristic of Hank to try to ignore anything that challenges the validity of his own point of view. Convinced that the Church is evil, he finds good priests "disagreeable" because they offer disturbing evidence that he may be mistaken. He recognizes that "the great majority" of the clergy "were sincere and right-hearted, and devoted to the alleviation of human troubles and sufferings," but he makes a point of thinking about the implications of this knowledge as seldom as possible.

Indeed, for all the attacks Hank makes upon the Church, it is significant that we are not supplied with supporting evidence within the text. We hear a lot about the wickedness of the clergy, but rarely do we get to meet any of them. And when we finally do get to meet a priest, he is performing an act of charity. In chapter thirty-five, a young woman is about to be executed. She holds her baby in her arms, even as the noose is placed around her neck, "devouring the baby all the time, wildly kissing it, and snatching it to her breast, and drenching it with tears." A priest is there to comfort her, and when the woman cries out that her child will die, lacking a father, mother, or home, she is reassured to the contrary: "'It has them all!' said that good priest. 'All these will I be to it till I die.'"

Hank claims that he opposes the Church because he believes in the separation of church and state. But he nevertheless proceeds on his own to foster religions more to his taste. One of his first acts as "The Boss" is to establish "a complete variety of Protestant congregations" so that everybody "could be any kind of Christian he wanted to be." The irony here is twofold. On the one hand, Hank reveals an attitude toward religion that is extraordinarily casual—he assumes that none of the differences among Christians are of any consequence. To urge men to be "any kind of Christian" is to accept the idea of being a poor Christian whenever it is convenient, in business dealings, for example. On the other hand, Hank's seemingly "liberal" stance is not as liberal as it pretends to be. His conception of "religious freedom" is not so generous as to allow for the possibility of being anything else but Christian—of one sort or another. A Connecticut Yankee through and through, it never occurs to him that Jews are people too.

The language that Hank uses to describe the clergy clearly reveals that, however noble his principles, Hank is really a bigot at heart. For example, he describes a monastary as "vomiting monks and nuns," and he portrays a group of pilgrims as "a herd." When a hermit dies, Hank regrets that "this animal would now be dubbed a martyr." And ultimately he makes a damaging confession about his opposition to the Church these men and women represent: "I had no scruples, but was willing to assault it in any way or with any weapon that promised to hurt it."

Such thinking as this prepares the way for Hank's "final solution." His blind determination to blame the Church for all that is wrong in society is characteristic of the modern authoritarian mind. He is the victim not so much of the Church but of the idea that

all the evils of social experience are attributable to a scape-goat class—the serious belief that if only one destroys the capitalist class, or the Jews, or, in the Yankee's case, destroys the aristocracy and/or the church, Utopia will follow as a matter of course. Such an idea is apt . . . to lead to mass slaughter—to genocide—and the Battle of the Sand Belt is precisely an act of genocide.[18]

Just as the textual evidence reveals that Hank Morgan is an unreliable judge of the Church, so does it suggest that Hank's contempt for chivalry is one-sided and narrow-minded. Although Hank tells us that King Arthur's blood was "rotten with unconscious brutality," there are at least two scenes that suggest Arthur possesses true nobility of character. The king does not hesitate to enter a hut infested with smallpox in order to help the dying woman and child found within, and even Hank is moved to momentary admiration:

Here was heroism at its last and loftiest possibility, its utmost summit; this was challenging death in the open field unarmed, with all the odds against the challenger, no reward set upon the contest, and no admiring world . . . to gaze and applaud. . . . He was great now; sublimely great.

Later, after both men have been captured as slaves, Hank is impressed by the way Arthur preserves his dignity even as a slave. The slavemaster is irritated by the way the king carries himself, and he beats him badly.

at the end of a week there was plenty of evidence that lash and club and fist had done their work well; the king's body was a sight to see—and to weep over; but his spirit—why, it wasn't even phased. Even that dull clod of a slave driver was able to see that there can be such a thing as a slave who will remain a man till he dies; whose bones you can break, but whose manhood you can't.

Even in rags, Arthur still looks like a king. But Hank is
incapable of understanding the significance of what he
observes. The victim of his own "inherited ideas," he
will declare war upon chivalry only a few pages later.
And the basis of his antagonism is an argument the
book has proven to be untrue—the argument that,
"barring clothes," there are no differences among men,
and if he were to strip the nation naked, a stranger
"couldn't tell the king from a quack doctor, nor a duke
from a hotel clerk."

In short, Hank Morgan never learns. He arrives in
Camelot with all the prejudices of a nineteenth-century
provincial. He encounters a civilization that is radically
different from his own—a civilization that is, without
question, far from perfect. But his understanding of
that civilization never grows in either depth or complexity. He is, in Twain's own words, "a perfect igno-
ramus,"[19] and his opinions cannot be accepted at face
value.

It would be a mistake, however, to read *A Connecticut Yankee in King Arthur's Court* as a satire at
Hank's sole expense. Twain satirizes modern industrial
society through Hank, whose faith in advertising and
cost effectiveness is naive to say the least. But Twain is
no simple romantic. Throughout the nineteenth century, many writers glorified the Middle Ages, finding
within the distant past a soothing contrast to the dark
Satanic mills they saw before them. From Sir Walter
Scott—who, as we know, Twain absolutely loathed—
on to Carlyle, Ruskin, and the Pre-Raphaelites, the
Gothic Revival in architecture, and a resurgence in
Arthurian scholarship that continues to this day, postindustrial man has been fascinated by the Age of Chivalry and Faith. But *A Connecticut Yankee* is not a part
of this tradition. Hank's condemnation of Camelot is
excessive, and through it we discover many of his lim-

itations. On the other hand, it must also be acknowledged that Twain was not trying to idealize the past.

Speaking in Baltimore in 1889—the year in which
A Connecticut Yankee was published—Twain empha-
sized the progress that man had made since the Middle
Ages:

Conceive the blank and sterile ignorance of that day, and
contrast it with the vast and many-sided knowledge of this.
Consider the trivial miracles and wonders wrought by the
humbug magicians and enchanters of that old day, and contrast them with the mighty miracles wrought by science in
our day of steam and electricity.[20]

Whatever the limitations of a Hank Morgan, a Morgan
Le Fay is by no means an ideal alternative. We sympathize with the prisoners we meet in her dungeons, and
throughout the novel, we sympathize with the poor
and oppressed in general. If Twain satirized the limitations of his own contemporaries, he also satirized the
modern tendency to be nostalgic about the past. His
past is a past filled with slaves, squalor, and superstition.

But Twain's presentation of the Middle Ages is
highly colored by his knowledge of more recent history. For the scenes involving slaves, he drew heavily
upon the work of Charles Bell, *Fifty Years in Chains or
the Life of an American Slave,* prompting one critic to
observe that Camelot "becomes on closer inspection a
wretched Arkansas village plus a castle."[21] Twain was
also influenced by Carlyle's *French Revolution* and
Lecky's *History of European Morals.* Recent scholarship has shown that some of the most pathetic scenes
in *A Connecticut Yankee*—the scene, for example, in
which a woman is executed for stealing a piece of
cloth—can be traced to these two works. So Twain's
version of Camelot may seem more candid than what
we find in Tennyson or William Morris, but it cannot
be accepted as accurate. As Twain acknowledged in

his original preface to the novel: "My object has been to group together some of the most odious laws which have had vogue in the Christian countries within the past eight or ten centuries, and illustrate them by the incidents of a story."

Therefore, *A Connecticut Yankee in King Arthur's Court* should not be read as an attack upon the Middle Ages per se, any more than as a satire of modern American values. It is, as Twain himself reminded us, a *contrast*. The contrast between the medieval and the modern is comic in so far as it is grotesque—neither the past nor the present is any more ideal than human nature itself. If humor seems eventually to disappear toward the end of the novel, it is because the apocalyptic conclusion denies us the possibility of hope. Presented with a vision of history in which corruption seems to triumph, a vision in which the present is but a logical extension of the past, we are ultimately left scorched by Twain's anger at the perpetual stupidity of men. As Hank Morgan observes, almost certainly speaking for Twain: "I reckon we are all fools. Born so, no doubt."

6

The Imitation White:
Pudd'nhead Wilson

As recently as 1955, F. R. Leavis could complain that it was difficult to find anyone who had read *Pudd'nhead Wilson*.[1] Since then, an increasing number of readers have been attracted to this complex tale of miscegenation in the American South. Its meaning has proved elusive; some critics see the work as a "classically conceived tragedy,"[2] while others view it as "an impressive comic triumph."[3] But despite radically different interpretations, there now exists a widespread consensus that *Pudd'nhead Wilson* is "one of the best late-nineteenth-century American novels,"[4] second only to *Huckleberry Finn* in terms of Twain's own accomplishment.

We return once again to the Mississippi River valley of Twain's youth. On the first of February 1830, two baby boys are born in the house of Percy Driscoll, one of the principal citizens of Dawson's Landing, Missouri. One of these children, christened Thomas à Becket, is heir to the Driscoll fortune; the other is the son of one of the family's slaves, a beautiful woman named Roxana. Following the death of Mrs. Percy Driscoll a week after her confinement, Roxy becomes responsible for taking care of both children.

Roxy is only one-sixteenth black, but Twain quickly reminds us that "the one-sixteenth of her which was black out-voted the other fifteen parts and made her a negro. She was a slave, and saleable as such." She calls her son Valet de Chambre, having "heard the phrase somewhere; the fine sound of it had pleased her ear, and as she had supposed it was a name, she loaded it on to her darling." Although only one-thirty-second black, Chambers—as he comes to be called—is still a slave and "by a fiction of law and custom, a negro." Nonetheless, he has blue eyes and a fair complexion and can be told from the Driscoll baby only by his clothes.

Finding himself the victim of petty thievery, Percy Driscoll threatens to sell his slaves down the river unless they confess their guilt. Three of them promptly do so, and Driscoll contents himself with selling them to other owners in the district—a "noble and gracious" decision that leaves him "privately well pleased with his magna-nimity." Innocent of wrongdoing, Roxy remains Dris-coll's property, as does her seven-month-old son. But, having witnessed the ease with which slaves can be sold, Roxy is now possessed by "a profound terror." Fearing that her son may live only to be sold down the river someday, she plans to throw herself into the Mississippi, her child in her arms. Determined to look well in death, she puts on a new Sunday gown and then dresses Chambers in an outfit that belongs to her master's child. She is struck anew by the similarity between the two babies, and after clothing Thomas à Becket in the coarse linen shirt of a slave, she declares, "Dog my cats if it ain't all *I* kin do to tell t'other fum which, let alone his pappy." She abandons any thought of suicide, se-cure now in the knowledge that her son has exchanged places with the boy who might otherwise have been his master. From this bold act, the plot unfolds.

No one in Dawson's Landing detects the switch that Roxy has made, not even David Wilson, a local attorney nicknamed "Pudd'nhead" by the people of the town— unable to appreciate his ironic humor, they have convinced themselves that he must be simple. Afflicted by this reputation as a fool, Wilson has no clients; he passes his time observing his fellow citizens and collecting their fingerprints, a "hobby" that the town takes as a further mark of his eccentricity. Although he had fingerprinted both babies shortly after their birth, and does so again after Roxy has "rechristened" them, Wilson—like the rest of the town—accepts the son of a slave as a legitimate heir to Percy Driscoll, while the true heir is relegated to the slave quarters.

Roxana's child, now called Tom Driscoll, grows up to be spoiled, selfish, and mean—sometimes to the point of brutality. The real Thomas Driscoll, now known as the slave Chambers, is "meek and docile," but he is also physically strong and remains loyal to his master even though he is regularly beaten without cause.

Shortly before he dies in 1845, Percy Driscoll sells Chambers to his brother, Judge York Driscoll. Tom goes to live with his "uncle," and learns that the old man intends to leave him all his property. And, set free by Percy's will, Roxy leaves Dawson's Landing in order to work on a steamboat.

By the time Tom is twenty-one, he has become a compulsive gambler, sneaking off to St. Louis where he runs up large debts. The Judge is disgusted with Tom's behavior and frequently threatens to disinherit him. When Tom eventually realizes that he can no longer expect his uncle to pay his debts for him, he becomes a thief, dressing up as a woman and breaking into the homes of his fellow citizens.

After working for eight years as a chambermaid on a steamboat, Roxy plans to retire since she is suffering from rheumatism. But the bank to which she has entrusted her savings suddenly collapses, leaving her penniless. She decides to return to Dawson's Landing and ask Tom to help her, convinced that he would be willing to spare a dollar a month for the woman who had been his "mammy," even though he is unaware that she is actually a good deal more to him. When she does so, however, Tom won't hear of it: "A dollar!— give you a dollar! I've a notion to strangle you! Is *that* your errand here? Clear out! and be quick about it!"

Roxy is enraged by such callous treatment, and she reveals to Tom his true identity. In order to keep her from making her knowledge public, Tom promises to pay his mother twenty-five dollars a month. Together, they form an alliance of a sort, with Roxy helping to mastermind the robberies that are still necessary to pay off Tom's ever-present gambling debts.

At about the same time that Roxy returns to Dawson's Landing, two identical twins named Luigi and Angelo Capello come to settle in the town. They are, we are told, Italian aristocrats—and they prove themselves to be courteous, well-educated, and musically talented. They represent, in short, almost everything that Tom Driscoll is not. A rivalry quickly develops, and the twins seem destined to usurp the social leadership of the town. When Tom publicly insults them, Luigi responds by kicking Tom off the platform on which they had been standing.

Tom thereupon takes Luigi to court on a charge of assault and battery. Judge Driscoll is horrified. According to his code, a gentleman never asks the law to settle his disputes; he settles them himself on a "field of honor." Humiliated by Tom's cowardice, the Judge challenges Luigi to a duel, but both men escape unhurt.

Shortly after this incident, Tom decides to rob his own uncle, and Judge Driscoll discovers him in the act. Recognizing that he would certainly be disinherited if his uncle lived, Tom kills the Judge—but not before he is able to cry out for help.

Luigi and Angelo had been walking near the house,

and hearing this cry, they rush inside to see what is the matter. They are discovered standing over the Judge's body. And given the enmity already known to have existed between the two brothers and the murdered man, they are arrested for the Driscoll murder. It seems certain that they will hang, but they insist upon their innocence and hire David Wilson as their attorney.

Wilson determines that the fingerprints on the murder weapon belong to neither twin, but he knows that this observation alone—at a time when fingerprinting was not yet commonly understood—would never convince a jury that his clients are innocent. Since his house is next-door to Judge Driscoll's, Wilson had once seen a mysterious young woman in Tom Driscoll's bedroom. He wonders if this woman might not prove to be the judge's murderer, and he tries to match the fingerprints on the knife with which the murder had been committed with the fingerprints he has collected over the years. He limits himself, however, to the fingerprints of women, unaware that the "woman" he had seen was really Tom Driscoll in the disguise he wore when stealing.

On the night before the trial is expected to end, Tom visits Wilson and teases him about his failure. He picks up one of the glass plates that Wilson uses to record fingerprints, and when the lawyer looks at it, he immediately realizes that Tom is the murderer. After Tom leaves, Wilson examines the other prints he has taken of Tom over the years, and he discovers that they do not match with those that he had taken of him as a baby. He has discovered, in short, Tom's true identity, and he establishes it in court, conclusively proving that Judge Driscoll was murdered by a slave masquerading as his nephew.

The twins are released and return to Europe, "weary of Western adventure." Chambers is restored to his rightful position. And Tom is sentenced to life imprisonment. The creditors of the late Percy Driscoll protest, however, that this is a waste of valuable property. "Everybody saw that there was reason in this. Everybody granted that if 'Tom' were white and free it would be unquestionably right to punish him—it would be no loss to anybody; but to shut up a valuable slave for life—that was another matter." The Governor thereupon pardons Tom, and the creditors sell him down the river—precisely the fate that his mother had tried to spare him when she tried to change his identity.

There are many problems with this plot. For one thing, it is never made clear why two Italian noblemen would choose to settle in a small town in Missouri; their story seems arbitrarily drawn into what is essentially an American story. Nor is it clear why David Wilson chooses to remain in Dawson's Landing for twenty years during which he cannot secure a single client, supporting himself through the sort of minor clerical work that must have been both boring and humiliating to someone clever enough to write the maxims that preface each chapter.[5] Moreover, the plot relies upon coincidence to an unlikely degree: Roxy happens to lose her savings; the twins happen to pass the Driscoll house at the very moment of the murder; and Tom just happens to leave behind an incriminating fingerprint only hours before the trial is about to end. Underlying all this is still another coincidence—a coincidence without which the story would be impossible: two boys are born in the same house on the same day, and they bear a remarkable similarity.

The plot is more easily understood when we realize that *Pudd'nhead Wilson* was originally conceived as a farce entitled "Those Extraordinary Twins." Fascinated by a newspaper account of Italian Siamese twins who were touring the United States, Twain set out to write a "fantastic little story" in which this "freak of nature" would inspire various comic episodes. He himself provides an excellent account of what happened as he wrote:

> But the tale kept spreading along, and spreading along, and other people got to intruding themselves and taking up more and more room with their talk and their affairs. Among them came a stranger named Pudd'nhead Wilson, and a woman named Roxana; and presently the doings of these two pushed up into prominence a young fellow named Tom Driscoll, whose proper place was away in the obscure background. Before the book was half finished those three were taking things almost entirely into their own hands and working the whole tale as a private venture of their own—a tale which they had nothing at all to do with, by rights.

Twain was unhappy with the result because "it was not one story, but two stories tangled together; and they obstructed and interrupted each other at every turn and created no end of confusion and annoyance." Recognizing that the two stories were incompatible, Twain reports that he "pulled one of the stories out by the roots, and left the other one—a kind of literary Caesarean operation."[6]

But this is something of an exaggeration. Twain did not remove his original story "by the roots." Luigi and Angelo Capello are left behind, although they are no longer Siamese twins. This makes their presence in Dawson's Landing more difficult to understand, and the account they provide of their background only heightens the confusion. Angelo remarks that "Our parents could have made themselves comfortable by exhibiting us as a show," and he reports that, after the parents die, the two boys were "placed among the attractions of a cheap museum in Berlin." None of this makes much sense now that Twain has deprived them of their deformity. It is true that the twins will be made to serve a useful function in the plot, but there is no reason why they have to be particularly exotic in order to do so. They don't even have to be Italian, and Twain admits as much: "They had no occasion to have foreign names now, but it was too much trouble to remove them all through, so I left them christened as they were and made no explanation." In short, Twain's story is marred by the same sort of careless editing that characterizes so much of his work.

But despite its improbability, the plot of *Pudd'n-head Wilson* reveals a definite design. The novel is built around the opposition between a series of pairs. The tradition-bound Judge Driscoll befriends the ironic David Wilson, and they form between them the only two members of the local Freethinkers' Society. When the prosperous judge is murdered, the impecunious attorney rises to prominence. More importantly, Tom's fate is linked to Chambers's just as Luigi's is to Angelo's. And through the complications of the plot, Tom is also matched against Luigi.[7] One man's success demands another man's loss. If the twins are found innocent of having killed Judge Driscoll, it is only because the true murderer has been caught, and if Chambers lives to recover his patrimony, it is only because Tom has been sold down the river. The conflict among these characters illustrates the dichotomy of life in the American South. Through the opposition of true gentleman versus false, slave-owner versus slave, and ultimately white versus black, Twain is able to explore fundamental questions of identity.

Dawson's Landing is dominated by a small group of "gentlemen" who never question their identity. They see themselves as Southern aristocrats, pointing with pride to elaborate family genealogies. At first, Twain's attitude toward this class seems to be relatively sympathetic. Describing Judge Driscoll, he writes:

He was very proud of his old Virginian ancestry, and in his hospitalities and his rather formal and stately manners he kept up its traditions. He was fine and just and generous. To be a gentleman—a gentleman without stain or blemish—was his only religion, and to it he was always faithful.

And one leading critic of the work has gone so far as to conclude that Twain "unmistakably admires" Driscoll.[8] But, knowing what we do of Twain, it is much more likely that he is simply continuing, in a quieter key, the satire of Southern gentry that had enlivened both *Life on the Mississippi* and *The Adventures of Huckleberry Finn*.

Consider, for example, the following passage:

In Missouri a recognized superiority attached to any person who hailed from Old Virginia; and this superiority was exalted to supremacy when a person of such nativity could also prove descent from the First Families of that great commonwealth. The Howards and Driscolls were of this aristocracy. In their eyes it was a nobility. It had its unwritten laws, and they were as clearly defined and as strict as any that could be found among the printed statutes of the land. The F.F.V. was born a gentleman; his highest duty in life was to watch over that great inheritance and keep it unsmirched. He must keep his honor spotless. Those laws were his chart; his course was marked on it; if he swerved from it by so much as half a point of the compass it meant shipwreck to his honor; that is to say, degradation from his rank as a gentleman . . . . Honor stood first; and the laws defined what it was and wherein it differed in certain details from honor as defined by church creeds and by the social laws and customs of some of the minor divisions of the globe that had got crowded out when the sacred boundaries of Virginia were staked out.

Twain's attitude here is clearly ironic. The Virginian aristocracy is "nobility" only in "their eyes," not the author's. The reference to honor as "that great inheritance" also suggests a certain amount of distance on Twain's part. And the last sentence, juxtaposing "the minor divisions of the globe" against "the sacred boundaries of

Virginia," is less subtle; it makes the self-proclaimed "First Families" of Virginia seem extraordinarily provincial.

The characterization of Judge Driscoll in particular gives force to Twain's irony. When he learns that Tom had failed to challenge Luigi to the duel that honor demanded, the Judge "sank forward in a swoon," as if he had "received a death-stroke." There is something profoundly ludicrous about the social and political leader of the town fainting away at the first hint of a family scandal like a frail heroine in a Victorian melodrama.[9] And the language he uses when he recovers increases the sense that the Judge is making a fool of himself. "Say it ain't true," he declares to a friend, "tell me it ain't true!" Learning that the story is indeed true, Driscoll histrionically demands, "Oh, what have I done to deserve this infamy!" Such language as this borders on the comic; it is too trite and overblown to express genuine emotion.

The duel that then results between Judge Driscoll and Luigi Capello provides material for further satire. The inanity of dueling—a favorite subject of Twain's— is suggested by the dialogue that passes between the Judge and Pembroke Howard, the friend who has agreed to act as his second.

"Well, Howard—the news?"

"The best in the world."

"Accepts, does he?" and the light of battle gleamed joyously in the Judge's eye.

"Accepts? Why he jumped at it."

"Did, did he? Now that's fine—that's very fine. I like that. When is it to be?"

"Now! Straight off! Tonight! An admirable fellow—admirable!"

"Admirable? He's a darling! Why, it's an honor as well as a pleasure to stand up before such a man. Come—off with you! Go and arrange everything—and give him my heartiest compliments. A rare fellow, indeed; an admirable fellow, as you have said!"

The irony here is that the Judge is full of admiration for a man whom he is about to try to kill. One can only marvel at the absurdity of a code that would put a man in such a position.

What follows from this scene serves to emphasize the shallowness of the Southern code of honor. The duel itself is reduced to a farce in which nearly all the by-standers are injured while the participants remain un-hurt. And after the duel is over, Tom explains to his uncle that he wished he could have fought Luigi him-self, but that "no honorable person could consent to meet him in the field." He describes Luigi as "a con-fessed assassin," and the Judge accepts Tom's word for it without making any attempt to investigate. Because of the warmth of their reception in the town, the twins had decided to run for public office, and the Judge now devotes himself to attacking them. He denounces them as "side-show riff-raff" and "dime-museum freaks." His high conception of "honor" does not keep him from fighting a dirty political campaign in which he sides with someone whose word he has good reason to doubt and slanders two men he had recently befriended.[10]

More disturbingly, the honor upon which men like the Judge so pride themselves does not keep them from having sexual relations with their slaves—possi-bly by force. At no point does anyone in the town's elite question the morality of owning one's own flesh and blood, to say nothing of the morality of slavery in itself. Their belief in chivalry brings with it the uncriti-cal acceptance of a feudal *droit de seigneur*. And the entire story of *Pudd'nhead Wilson* hinges upon the fact that generations of miscegenation had made it impossi-ble to tell a free man from a slave except by "a fiction of law and custom."

Thus while Judge Driscoll may be "a fairly humane man towards slaves and other animals," he is by no means as honorable as he thinks he is. His identity is false. It originates in self-deception and is established through fraud. If he is publicly perceived to be a gentleman, it is because the inhabitants of Dawson's Landing believe what they are told. Twain observes that "irony was not for those people; their mental vision was not focused for it." As a result, they are unable to see the discrepancy between the aristocratic code and the injustice it tolerates. They accept the town's elite at its own valuation, believing themselves fortunate to have such men among them: "The people took more pride in the duel than in all the other events put together perhaps. It was a glory to their town to have such a thing happen there." Given their unreasoning belief in the values with which they have been presented, the town's people cannot tell appearance from reality. Confusing identity with public image, they accept people at face value, making serious mistakes as they do so—the most serious of which is their failure to see Tom Driscoll for what he is: a liar, a thief, and eventually a murderer. He is, in their eyes, "the Judge's nephew," and as such above reproach.

The arrival of Luigi and Angelo Capello underscores the fact that the local gentry have assumed an identity that is not rightfully theirs. The Driscolls and the Howards pretend to be aristocrats, but their inadequacies are emphasized when titled Europeans come to town. The average citizen is overwhelmed:

None of them had ever seen a person bearing a title of nobility before, and none had been expecting to see one now, consequently the title came upon them as a kind of pile-driving surprise, and caught them unprepared. A few tried to rise to the emergency, and got out an awkward 'My lord', or 'Your lordship', or something of that sort, but the great majority were overwhelmed by the unaccustomed word and its dim and

awful associations with gilded courts and stately ceremony
and annointed kingship, so they only fumbled through the
handshake and passed on, speechless.

Acquaintance with descendents from the First Families
of Virginia has been no preparation for a moment like
this. And Judge Driscoll himself is one of the guests at
the reception, where he is quick to compete for friendship with the twins. We learn that he had "the good fortune to secure them for an immediate drive, and to be
the first to display them in public." If there is a hint of
vulgarity in the alacrity with which the Judge pursues
the twins, his crudeness is obvious when we learn what
he does with his guests.

The Judge showed the strangers the new graveyard, and the
gaol, and where the richest man lived, and the Freemasons'
Hall, and the Methodist Church, and the Presbyterian Church,
and where the Baptist Church was going to be. . . .

From there the party goes on to inspect the town hall
and the slaughterhouse, a tour that could hardly have excited visitors who arrive in Missouri by way of Venice,
London, Paris, Russia, India, China, and Japan. Seen
beside the twins, Judge Driscoll can be understood for
what he is: a self-important provincial who is thoroughly at home in "a slaveholding town, with a rich,
slave-worked grain and pork country back of it."

But Twain is not simply interested in ridiculing the
pretensions of a particular social class. He draws our
attention to the hypocrisy of the Southern gentleman
only because it illustrates the dishonesty he sees beneath the attractive surface of American life. The "aristocratic" sense of identity may be based upon a lie, but
it is not the only case of mistaken identity to be found
in *Pudd'nhead Wilson*. David Wilson is misperceived
as a fool; the twins are falsely accused of murder; and
Tom dresses up as a girl in order to rob the homes of
his friends.

More seriously, Roxy is able to "pass" as a white. And her child is able to convince the world that he is not only "white" but also a "gentleman," leading us to realize that the identification of Americans as either "white" or "black" is both idiotic and corrupt. Tom and Chambers are able to assume false identities primarily because their original identities, as defined by society, do not reflect the reality of who they are. But to appreciate the significance of this theme, we must take a closer look at what the novel has to say about race.

After Tom learns the secret of his birth, he asks himself:

Why were niggers *and* whites made? What crime did the un-created first nigger commit that the curse of birth was decreed for him? And why is this awful difference made between white and black? . . . How hard the nigger's fate seems, this morning!—yet until last night such a thought never entered my head.

Tom had never really thought about blacks since he had always taken them for granted; slaves, in his eyes, were simply another form of animal. It is necessary for him to *become* "black" in order for him to even begin to understand what this means—just as Hank Morgan and King Arthur had to become slaves before they could experience disenfranchisement in medieval Britain. Unfortunately, Tom's values are so firmly fixed that he cannot profit from his knowledge. Although Twain concedes that several of Tom's opinions change, he insists that "the main structure of his character was not changed and could not be changed." Twenty-one years of conditioning cannot be overcome, and Tom continues to think like a white.[11] Thus when his mother tells him that she loves him, "It made him wince, secretly—for she was a 'nigger'. That he was one himself was far from reconciling him to that despised race."

This results in a curious split in identity—a "black" who thinks that he is "white" because that is what he has been taught. The society in which he lives demands that he be either one or the other. This dilemma is responsible for Tom's anguished demand, "Why were niggers *and* whites made?" It is important to note the emphasis that is given to the conjunction. As a recent critic has convincingly argued:

For Mark Twain, the tragedy is not in being born black, but in being born black into a white world. . . . Man's punishment lies in the very fragmentation of his physical as well as moral nature. The contrast between white and black with all its symbolic and cosmic connotations of struggle and strife lives in the flesh of man.[12]

The reality of this struggle is more apt to be felt by blacks, however, than by whites, who form, after all, the comfortable majority. Blacks, on the other hand, must contend with the knowledge that their color has been seen as a mark of inferiority; they are the "despised race" in the eyes of the Tom Driscolls of the world.

In order to survive in a white world, Twain's blacks acquire "all the wheedling and supplicating servilities that fear and interest can impart to the words and attitudes of the born slave." They know what is expected of them, and they are anxious to conform. Twain acknowledges that blacks can be loyal to one another. When Roxy is in trouble, another slave slips her a roasted potato, and she is later protected by free men and women on board a steamboat. But he emphasizes that blacks are partially responsible for their own oppression. Tom sells his own mother back into slavery, and one could not ask for a more vivid example of someone betraying his own kind. And when Roxy subsequently attacks a vicious overseer "en laid him flat," all the other field hands choose to remain in bondage while she alone makes for the river—in her words, "de niggers 'uz plum sk'yered to death.

Dey gathered 'round him to he'p him . . . ." Twain marvels at the willingness of the oppressed to assist their oppressors, implying that the system under which they suffer would not be possible without their cooperation.[13]

Of all Twain's characters, Roxy is one of the most interesting. She is presented to us at first in terms that make her almost heroic: "She was of majestic form and stature; her attitudes were imposing and statuesque, and her gestures and movements distinguished by a noble and stately grace." And this description is justified when we consider some of her acts. It takes a very bold woman to switch two babies in their cradles, and then keep the secret for over twenty years. She is, among other things, wonderfully brave—as evidenced not only by her escape from slavery but also by her refusal to be intimidated by her wealthy son:

Does you think you kin skyer me? It ain't in you, nor in de likes of you. I reckon you'd shoot me in de back, maybe, if you got a chance, for dat's jist yo' style—*I* knows you, thoo en thoo—but I don't mind gitt'n killed . . . .

Such a speech as this is reminiscent more of Colonel Sherburn than of Aunt Polly, and it would be fair to say that Roxy stands alone, among Twain's women, as the corporeal equal of men. But she can also be magnificently maternal, as shown by her willingness to be sold back into slavery in order to help Tom pay his debts. It is impossible not to feel the strength of her words:

Ain't you my chile? En does you know anything dat a mother won't do for her chile? Dey ain't nothin' a white mother won't do for her chile. Who made 'em so? De Lord done it. En who made de niggers? De Lord made 'em. In de inside, mothers is all de same.

Admirable though this speech is, it nonetheless reflects Roxy's principal weakness. She sees herself competing with white mothers and trying to equal what she believes that they would do. She is, in short, too eager to model herself on whites. This is seen most clearly when she discovers that Tom has refused to fight Luigi in a duel. Her bitterness echoes Judge Driscoll's:

En you refuse' to fight a man dat kicked you, 'stid o' jumpin at de chance! En you ain't got no mo' feelin' den to come en tell me, dat fetched sich a po' low-down ornery rabbit into de worl'! Pah! it makes me sick! It's de nigger in you, dat's what it is. Thirty-one parts o' you is white, en on'y one part nigger, en dat po' little one part is yo' *soul*. 'Tain't wuth savin'; tain't wuth totin' out on a shovel en thrown' in de gutter. You has disgraced you' birth. What would yo' pa think o' you? It's enough to make him turn in his grave.

As this speech suggests, Roxy is no black militant. She is convinced that whites are superior to blacks and that Tom's cowardice can be traced only to the "nigger" in him, and not to any of his many white ancestors. When she says that he has disgraced his birth, she means that he has disgraced the white slaveholders with whom she has been lucky enough to sleep.

Indeed, Roxy shares the values of the Southern gentry to the extent of making them unintentionally comic. Boasting of her ancestry to Tom, she sounds like a grotesque parody of the Judge:

Whatever has come o' yo' Essex blood? Dat's what I can't understan'. En it ain't on'y jist Essex blood dat's in you, not by a long sight—'deed it ain't! My great-great-great-gran'-father en yo' great-great-great-great-gran'-father was ole Cap'n John Smith, de highest blood dat Ole Virginny ever turned out, en *his* great-great-gran'mother, or somers along back dah, was Pocahontas de Injun queen, en her husbun' was a nigger king outen Africa.

It is almost certain that Twain intended us to smile at the absurdity of this speech. But there is something serious going on here, as the following scene makes clear. Roxy has just returned to Dawson's Landing after an eight-year absence. She is sitting in the Driscoll kitchen, gossiping with the family's slaves, when she learns that Tom has been temporarily disinherited. She demands, of Chambers, what this means:

> "Dissen*whiched* him?"
> "Dissenhurrit him."
> "What's dat? What does it mean?"
> "Means he by'sted de will."
> "Bu's—ted de will! He wouldn't *ever* treat him so! Take it back, you mis'able imitation nigger dat I bore in sorrow en tribbilation . . ."
> "Yah-yah-yah! Jes listen to dat! If I's imitation, what is you? Bofe of us is imitation *white*—dat's what we is—en pow'ful good imitation too—yah-yah-yah!—we don't 'mount to noth'n as imitation *niggers* . . . ."

On one level, Twain is deriving humor from this scene; both Roxy and Chambers speak in the comic dialect of the minstrel show, and a white nineteenth-century audience could be expected to laugh at one black calling another "nigger," just as they would laugh at Roxy's difficulty with "disinherit" and her inappropriate lapse into fundamentalist rhetoric. Nevertheless, the scene is ultimately serious. Roxy's willingness to call Chambers a "nigger" reveals a tragic flaw in her character—identifying herself with white slaveholding society, she intends "imitation nigger" to be deeply insulting. Chambers, on the other hand, is perfectly correct to point out to her that he is not an "imitation nigger" so much as an "imitation white." That's his problem, and it is Roxy's problem as well. They are caught between two cultures, a part of neither.

The conclusion of the novel emphasizes this point. After "Tom" is sold down the river, "Chambers" is restored to the position he had lost when he was seven months old. But psychologically, he is more dispossessed than ever:

The real heir suddenly found himself rich and free, but in a most embarrassing situation. He could neither read nor write, and his speech was the basest dialect of the negro quarter. His gait, his attitudes, his gestures, his bearing, his laugh—all were vulgar and uncouth; his manners were the manners of a slave. Money and fine clothes could not mend these defects or cover them up, they only made them the more glaring and the more pathetic. The poor fellow could not endure the terrors of the white man's parlor, and he felt home and at peace nowhere but in the kitchen. The family pew was a misery to him, yet he could nevermore enter into the solacing refuge of the "nigger gallery"—that was closed to him for good and all.

Chambers may now know who he is, but he cannot grasp what is expected of him. Mistaken identity has yielded to confused identity. He had seen himself as "imitation white" when he believed himself to be a slave who was only one-thirty-second black. Now publicly recognized as "white," he is condemned to act out a role for which he was not prepared. Ironically, he is now, more than ever before, an "imitation white."

Readers who are dissatisfied with this denouement should realize that Twain was not writing an Abolitionist tract in which new myths are allowed to take the place of the old. To show a slave finding instant happiness upon emancipation might comfort those who believe social ills can be easily corrected, but it would not do justice to the complexity of the problem at hand. And history has proven Twain to be right. Blacks have *not* found it easy to integrate themselves into a predominantly white culture. Their task has been impeded by the reluctance of American society to recognize its true children, but it has also been complicated by the persistence of the quandary that afflicts Chambers. Men and women continue to ask themselves what it means to be black, what it means to be white, and—those questions aside—to what extent can one retain a black identity after penetrating "the terrors of the white man's parlor."

Moreover, Twain did not dismiss the myth of the Southern gentleman only to replace it with the myth of the noble black. His slaves are idealized no more than their masters. Although Twain is unquestionably sympathetic to the plight of American blacks, he is not prepared to romanticize his characters in order to make a point. Taken as a whole, *Pudd'nhead Wilson* is remarkable for the evenhandedness with which the author treats the problem of black/white relations. Consider, for example, the passage in which he describes the petty larceny that slaves occasionally indulged in:

They had an unfair show in the battle of life, and they held it no sin to take military advantage of the enemy—in a small way; in a small way, but not in a large one. They would smouch provisions from the pantry whenever they got a chance; or a brass thimble, or a cake of wax . . . or any other property of light value; and so far were they from considering such reprisals sinful, they would go to church and shout and pray their loudest and sincerest with their plunder in their pockets. A farm smoke-house had to be heavily padlocked, for even the colored deacon himself could not resist a ham when Providence showed him in a dream, or otherwise, where such a thing hung lonesome and longed for someone to love. But with a hundred hanging before him the deacon would not take two—that is, on the same night. On frosty nights the humane negro prowler would warm the end of a plank and put it under the cold claws of chickens roosting in a tree; a drowsy hen would step on to the comfortable board softly clucking her gratitude, and the prowler would dump her into his bag, and later into his stomach, perfectly sure that in taking this trifle from the man who daily robbed him of an inestimable treasure—his liberty—he was not committing any sin that God would remember against him in the Last Great Day.

Far removed from the sentimentality of a Harriet Beecher Stowe, the attitude that we find here is remarkably complex. There is humor in the presentation of both the deacon and the prowler. But if the former steals only one ham a night and the latter uses a warm board to woo the chicken he is about to devour, it is not because there is anything innately comic about blacks. Their behavior may not be strictly moral, but their lapses are trivial compared to the immorality of the system under which they suffer. Twain does not deny that slaves would "smouch provisions from the pantry" and "take military advantage of the enemy," but he insists that their sins are venial. They should be measured against the "inestimable treasure" of liberty that had been stolen from them in the "unfair show" called "the battle of life."

Striving for objectivity, Twain also takes pains to emphasize that slavery was an *American* dilemma and not a problem for the South alone. When Tom sells Roxy to a plantation down the river, both her mistress and her overseer prove to be Northerners who are far more brutal than any of the whites in Dawson's Landing. In Roxy's words:

Dat overseer wuz a Yank, too, outen New Englan', en anybody down South kin tell you what dat mean. *Dey* knows how to work a nigger to death, en dey knows how to whale 'em, too—whale 'em till dey backs is welted like a washboard.

Twain reminds us once again that we should avoid stereotypes, believing that we will always be at odds with one another if we persist in viewing the history of race relations in our country as a conflict between good blacks and wicked Southerners. He knows that the truth is not this simple.

It thus becomes clear that there are more subtle forms of false identity than masquerading as a woman or pretending to be a fool. The ways in which we are most likely to see ourselves are all shown to be meaningless, whether they be based on class, race, or geographical background. The gentleman is not gentle, and—in the case of Tom Driscoll—the white man is not white. The black man, for his part, is seldom as simple as he

may appear, and his very identity as "black" may be
determined only by "a fiction of law and custom."
When we consider that Tom begins the novel "black"
and enslaved, but becomes "white" and free by simply
changing his clothes, only to become a slave once again
after twenty years of social prominence, we must realize
the absurdity of identifying ourselves in terms of race.
And identities based on geography are shown to be just
as inadequate. Judge Driscoll's obsession with "Old Virginia" is unquestionably foolish, a point that is made
more forcefully by the way in which Twain challenges
Northern sanctimony later in the novel. If Virginians
pride themselves upon genealogies that are likely to be
false, Northerners tend to pride themselves for upholding a liberal piety that is equally false. Roxy's worst
suffering is at the hands of New Englanders, as we have
seen, and Tom himself is a product of Yale University.
Travel into the heart of the Deep South, and there you
will find New Haven. Geographical divisions are therefore arbitrary. To see ourselves as "Northern" or
"Southern" makes no more sense than to see ourselves
as "black" or "white."

   While conceding that "Twain's own judgment of
sexual relations between black and white . . . is not
explicitly stated," Leslie Fiedler argues that "there
seems no doubt that he regarded the union between
Roxy and Essex with a certain degree of horror, regarded it as a kind of fall—even in itself and a source
of doom to all involved."[14] But this misses the point.
Our problem, in America, is not miscegenation so
much as divisiveness. The "doom" that envelops the
characters is not the result of the union of black and
white so much as the failure to recognize the inevitabil-
ity of that union and accept the consequences. Nothing
in *Pudd'nhead Wilson* suggests that Twain wants to
keep the races apart—on the contrary, he wants us to
see the senselessness of those laws and customs that

classify Americans into groups that have become increasingly meaningless in a nation that is profoundly
mixed. We should remember that Roxy is herself the
product of miscegenation, and she is the most attractive character in the novel.

With this reading of the book in mind, it is now
possible to understand the seemingly absurd joke with
which it opens. David Wilson has just arrived in Dawson's Landing, and he is speaking to a group of townspeople when "an invisible dog began to yelp and
snarl." This leads to a dialogue that makes Wilson seem
to be a "pudd'nhead."

> "I wish I owned half of that dog."
> "Why?" somebody asked.
> "Because I would kill my half."

This answer astounds the town:

> "'Pears to be a fool."
> "'Pears?" said another. "*Is*, I reckon you better say."
> "Said he wished he owned *half* of the dog, the idiot,"
> said a third. "What did he reckon would become of the other
> half if he killed his half? Do you reckon he thought it would
> live?"
> "Why, he must have thought it . . . because if he hadn't
> thought it, he would have wanted to own the whole dog,
> knowing that if he killed his half and the other half died, he
> would be responsible for that half just the same as if he had
> killed that half instead of his own. Don't it look that way to
> you, gents?"

The modern reader is apt to sympathize with those earnest citizens who do not find Wilson's joke amusing—it
is, if anything, vaguely threatening. But as James Cox
has observed, "The terms of the joke become the terms
of the novel."[15] Tom Driscoll is regularly described as
a "cur," a "miserable dog," and a "low-down hound."
And the emergence of his true parentage means that he
becomes a saleable piece of property. He is only one-
thirty-second black, but it is no more possible to own a

thirty-second of a man than to own half a dog. Consequently, Tom is completely ruined. His white blood is indivisible from his black, and his whole being is sold down the river, just as the invisible dog would have died if Wilson had his original wish. In the succinct words of another critic:

Wilson's half-dog becomes a stern test of Southern attitudes. Men who are aghast at the prospect of the newcomer's killing a creature that may be only partially his property—a moral and legal crime, clearly—are daily accustomed to dealing with members of their own species on precisely the same terms. . . . the concept of blood-fractions, it seems, applies only to the Negro.[16]

The joke therefore reinforces what Twain has been at pains to teach us. That the book attacks slavery is beyond dispute. But it also reveals a more subtle theme: death comes not only from owning men but also from trying to divide them.

Pudd'nhead Wilson is almost entirely free of the authorial intrusion to which Twain was so often tempted. He does not preach to us within these pages, preferring to expose the cancer of the American body politic with a heretofore unmatched degree of ironic detachment. At the end of the novel we are left in a world in which nothing has been changed. Tom is sold into slavery; Wilson becomes mayor; and the twins go back to Europe. But the structure of society remains intact. In A Connecticut Yankee in King Arthur's Court, Twain had fantasized about revolution only to acknowledge its ultimate failure. In Pudd'nhead Wilson, he cannot even pretend that the social order can be changed. He simply shows us what is wrong with us and then turns away.

7

‮vvvvvvvvvvvvvvvvvvvvvvvvvvvvvvvvvvvvvvvvvvvvvvv‬

The Growth of a
Misanthrope: Representative
Short Fiction

To survey Twain's career is to realize that his work is remarkably consistent. Although humor eventually gives way to irony, as St. Petersburg turns into Dawson's Landing, the disillusioned voice of the 1890s could be heard much earlier by those who know how to listen. *Pudd'nhead Wilson* may be harsher than *A Connecticut Yankee*, and *Huckleberry Finn* more serious than *Tom Sawyer*. But as we have seen, an inescapable sense of isolation haunts *Life on the Mississippi* and even *Tom Sawyer*—that seemingly sunny and optimistic work written when life appeared to stretch before America's most famous humorist in an uninterrupted vista of public triumph and familial love.

Twain's short stories and novellas reveal the same pattern. They range from the farcical to the tragic—as burlesque yields to satire—and an almost Swiftean contempt for the weakness of human nature. But whether written early or late, their content is recognizably Twain's. Frequently violent and almost always grotesque, the short fiction of Mark Twain recapitulates the concerns that dominate the major works.

In 1865, at the age of thirty, Twain published his first story to win national acclaim, "The Celebrated Jumping Frog of Calaveras County," a comic tale in which the nineteenth century found a degree of hilar-

ity now difficult to imagine. Its plot is simple: A fellow
named Jim Smiley makes a bet that his frog, Dan'l
Webster, can outjump any frog matched against it by
an unnamed stranger who is passing through town.
Smiley is confident he will win, since his frog is a
champion jumper, and the stranger seems dull-witted.
But the stranger wins the bet by filling Dan'l Webster
full of buckshot when Smiley isn't looking.

Our taste in humor has changed in the past century, and few readers nowadays find this tale to be all
that amusing. It is interesting, however, because it
foreshadows one of Twain's favorite themes: the con-
man who gets outconned. Jim Smiley is kin to the
hucksters who dominate *Life on the Mississippi*; he is
Tom Sawyer outsmarted by David Wilson, the underestimated stranger who ultimately has his way over the
village hero. Moreover, the story is full of grim detail.
There is a "one-eyed cow that didn't have no tail, only
just a short stump," a bull dog that "limped off a piece
and laid down and died" after being defeated in a
fight with a dog with no hind legs, and a disease-ridden
horse that gets "excited and desperate" when forced to
race. All of these creatures were originally meant to inspire laughter, but now that the laughter has died
away, we are left with a sense of rather morbid pathos.

Within ten years of writing this story, Twain transformed himself from an overworked journalist to a
successful man of letters. He was already settled in his
turreted Hartford mansion when he wrote "The Facts
Concerning the Recent Carnival of Crime in Connecticut" for the *Atlantic Monthly* in 1876. The narrator of
this story, a caricature of Twain, is sitting in his study
and smoking a cigar when the door opens and in walks
a "shrivelled, shabby dwarf," about two feet high and
so "out of shape" as to be "a deformity as a whole."
Covered all over with a "fuzzy, greenish mould, such
as one sometimes sees upon mildewed bread," he

strikes the narrator as a "vile bit of human rubbish."
But the dwarf also has a "foxlike cunning" in his face,
and his "sharp little eyes" are filled with malice. When
asked to identify himself, he explains that he is the narrator's conscience. With "exquisite cruelty," and enjoying himself thoroughly, the dwarf goes on to remind
the narrator of everything he has ever done wrong.

Demanding that he be addressed as "my lord," the
dwarf declares, "I am not your friend, I am your enemy; I am not your equal, I am your master." The
narrator asks if there is any way of satisfying him, and
the dwarf responds:

Ass! I don't care *what* act you may turn your hand to, I can
straightway whisper a word in your ear and make you think
you have committed a dreadful meanness. It is my *business*—
and my *joy*—to make you repent *everything* you do."

Tired of being tormented by his conscience, the narrator is eventually able to grab hold of the dwarf and kill
him:

With an exultant shout I sprang . . . and in an instant I had
my life-long foe by the throat. After so many years of waiting and longing, he was mine at last. I tore him to shreds and
fragments. I rent the fragments to bits. I cast the bleeding
rubbish into the fire, and drew into my nostrils the grateful
incense of my burnt-offering. At last, and forever, my Conscience was dead!

The narrator is now "a free man," and he tells us that
his new life is one of "unalloyed bliss":

Nothing in all the world could persuade me to have a conscience again. I settled all my old outstanding scores, and
began the world anew. I killed thirty-eight persons during
the first two weeks—all of them on account of ancient
grudges. I burned a dwelling that interrupted my view. I
swindled a widow and some orphans out of their last cow,
which is a very good one. . . . I have also committed scores
of crimes of various kinds, and have enjoyed my work ex-

ceedingly, whereas it would formerly have broken my heart
and turned my hair gray, I have no doubt.

Within the context of the story, all this is both humorous
and playful. The situation is so fantastic, the language
so archly melodramatic, and the crimes so exaggerated that even the most obtuse reader must realize
that he is having his leg pulled. Nevertheless, the fantasy around which the tale is built is central to many of
Twain's works. One month after writing "Carnival
of Crime in Connecticut," Twain began *The Adventures of Huckleberry Finn*—the climax of which is
Huck's decision to ignore his conscience and help
rescue Jim even if it means he will go to hell. Hank
Morgan later wishes, "If I had the remaking of man, he
wouldn't have any conscience." And much of the work
popularly known as *The Mysterious Stranger* is devoted to attacking conscience, or "the Moral Sense," as
it is there called. A comic tale about a man who kills his
conscience cannot, therefore, be taken altogether
lightly. Only the most self-important critics insist upon
the psychoanalysis of humor. But it should be noted
that Twain's treatment of this theme became more serious every time he returned to it.

"The Jumping Frog" and "The Carnival of
Crime" are both tall tales in the tradition of the American Southwest. But comparing the two stories reveals
Twain's growth. For the most part, "The Jumping
Frog" reflects an uncritical acceptance of local mores.
The author is at ease within the culture that gave him
his subject; there is no hint of Mark Twain as a social
philosopher. In "The Carnival of Crime," however, we
find Twain beginning to take issue with values his contemporaries held sacred. His attack upon conscience
may be oblique, but it is nonetheless subversive. With
the publication of this story, Twain "began to pit himself in imaginative opposition to the respectable community whose mores he had so eagerly adopted at the

beginning of the '70s and whose approval he had so anxiously cultivated,"[1] as Kenneth Lynn has pointed out.

"The Facts Concerning the Recent Carnival of Crime in Connecticut" was published the same year as *The Adventures of Tom Sawyer*. Much of the next decade would be devoted to the composition of *Huckleberry Finn*. It was published in 1885, and in that same year, Twain wrote a fictionalized memoir, which is one of the best of his shorter works, "The Private History of a Campaign That Failed." At a time when the public revered the men who had fought in the Civil War and might take their pick from dozens of memoirs chronicling the glories of war, Twain chose to challenge such values—not by playing the fool in the relative safety of burlesque, but by offering a quietly realistic account of boy-soldiers off the battlefield. The antecedent of more overt attacks upon war—like "To the Person Sitting in Darkness" and "The War Prayer"[2]— it attempts to explain why thousands of men "entered the war, got just a taste of it, and then stepped out permanently." As Twain observes in his introduction, the unheroic are entitled to a voice, "they ought at least be allowed to state why they didn't do anything. . . . Surely this kind of light must have a sort of value."

Twain tells us that he was in Hannibal when Missouri was invaded by Union forces in the summer of 1861 and the governor called out the militia to defend the state. Like Tom Sawyer's Gang, "Several of us got together in a secret place at night and formed ourselves into a military company." They call themselves the Marion Rangers and set out to do what they believe to be their duty. In the weeks that follow, the battalion spends most of its time in retreat, its principal concerns being staying dry and getting enough to eat. Because the men of the battalion are "hopeless material for war," not knowing how "to obey like machines," they fail as soldiers and ultimately disband. But they win our sympathy rather than our contempt. We come to know them as individuals who are recognizably human because they have not been buried beneath the trappings of heroic rhetoric.

Twain's comrades are all very young; they go to war not because they want to kill people but because it's exciting and romantic—like running away from home or playing at being pirates. A boy named Dunlap is responsible for christening the group the Marion Rangers; he was "young, ignorant, good-natured, well-meaning, trivial, full of romance, and given to reading chivalric novels and singing forlorn love-ditties." But no one finds fault with the name, and Twain himself "thought it sounded quite well." Like Dunlap, they see themselves as a band of dashing adventurers. Until the "steady trudging came to be like work," even marching was "all fun, all idle nonsense and laughter." And when they camp in "a shady and pleasant piece of woods," Twain remembers it as "an enchanting region for war—our kind of war." Going to war becomes a kind of adolescent folly, the result of innocence rather than brutality.

The novelty of their situation wears off, however, as the story unfolds. When it rains, Twain complains that "it took the romance all out of the campaign and turned our dreams of glory into a repulsive nightmare." And after about a week, Twain falls into the sort of melancholia that is found in so many of his works. Billeted with a farm family named Mason, Twain recalls that

after all these years the memory of the dullness and stillness and lifelessness of that slumberous farm-house still oppresses my spirit as with a sense of the presence of death and mourning. There was nothing to do, nothing to think about; there was no interest in life. The male part of the household were away in the fields all day, the women were busy and out of our sight; there was no sound but the plaintive wailing of a spinning-wheel, forever moaning out from some distant room,—the most lonesome sound in nature, a sound steeped and sodden with homesickness and the emptiness of life.[3]

But the tedium of such days is nothing compared to the anguish he experiences in the climax of the story when—in a wholly fictitious episode—Twain makes his first-person narrator kill an unarmed man, "a man who had never done me any harm." Unable to convince himself that this was "the enemy," Twain sounds very much like Huck when he tells us, "The thought of him got to preying upon me every night; I could not get rid of it." He knows, moreover, that he will be forced to kill again if he remains a soldier:

the taking of that unoffending life seemed such a wanton thing. And it seemed an epitome of war; that all war must be just that—the killing of strangers against whom you feel no personal animosity, strangers whom, in other circumstances, you would help if you found them in trouble. . . . My campaign was spoiled. It seemed to me that I was not rightly equipped for this awful business; that war was intended for men and I for a child's nurse.

Shortly afterward, he ends his brief military career, his war a "campaign that failed."

Twain occasionally drifts into the sort of farcical humor he found difficult to resist. In one scene, the battalion sleeps in a rat-infested corncrib; a rat bites someone on the toe, inspiring a fight that ends with everyone "locked in a death grip with his neighbor." But for the most part, "The Private History of a Campaign That Failed" avoids unnecessary exaggeration. Its tone is ironic, the narrator a man of experience looking back at an episode in his youth almost in surprise as he measures the distance that separates him from the past. One of the advantages of this tone is that it allows Twain to keep his audience with him through what amounts to an apologia for desertion. It is almost as if Twain is writing about someone else, someone he had known only in passing.

Mindful that his contemporaries might easily condemn his behavior as cowardly, Twain is careful not to sound self-righteous. While arguing that the thousands of men who avoided fighting in the war deserve a voice, he insists that this should be "not a loud one but a modest one, not a boastful one but an apologetic one." And he goes on to concede, "They ought not to be allowed much space among better people—people who did something." But this is a mock concession. A careful reading of the text reveals that Twain does not really consider those "who did something" to be "better people." If he treats his own lost innocence ironically, he is more ironic toward those who stayed in the war after he headed west. One of the members of the battalion is a boy named Smith:

This vast donkey had some pluck, of a slow and sluggish nature, but a soft heart; at one time he would knock a horse down for some impropriety, and at another he would get homesick and cry. However, he had one ultimate credit to his account which some of us hadn't; he stuck to the war, and was killed in battle at last.

The implication is that Smith stayed in the army because he was simpleminded; his greatest accomplishment seems to have been getting "killed in battle at last." If there is a possible hint of affection in describing him as a "vast donkey," there is none whatsoever in elsewhere describing the entire group as a "herd of cattle" and "rabbits." War reduces men to the level of beasts, and Twain sees nothing to boast about in this.

Most of the Marion Rangers are failures as soldiers, but Twain makes it clear that the well-trained are contemptible as well. He notes—as if defending the group—that "there were those among us who afterward learned the grim trade, learned to obey like machines, became valuable soldiers." This is ambivalent praise at best, and we are meant to ask ourselves if the master at "the grim trade" is really all that superior to the bumbling apprentice. The recruit may be an animal, but the veteran is an automaton. And as it retreats, Twain's battalion encounters a group of earnest young men being trained by their "fierce and profane" leader in the art of using a bowie knife like a machete. So far from being shamed by the example of more serious recruits, Twain observes, "It was a grisly spectacle to see that earnest band practising their murderous cuts and slashes under the eye of that remorseless old fanatic."

Twain's purpose in "A Campaign That Failed" is not, then, as simple as it purports to be. He is not really interested in explaining his own withdrawal from the war. It was not in question: Thousands of men had managed to escape service, many by the then-accepted practice of paying someone to take one's place. If Twain were only concerned with justifying his own record, his best recourse would have been to let it moulder in the obscurity that had already engulfed it. His real object is to question the legitimacy of war, stripping away the glory that obscures the reality of that "grim trade." That he did so at a time when both the war and Reconstruction were fresh in the minds of readers for whom patriotism was a cardinal virtue is a sign of Twain's alienation from the culture he had previously been content to amuse.

Compared to "The Carnival of Crime in Connecticut," "The Private History of a Campaign That Failed" is much more sophisticated. Ironic rather than humorous, it is much more subtle—and, as a result, more difficult to dismiss as literary high jinks. Twain has found the voice he would employ through the rest of his career—distant, mocking, and ultimately somber. This is the voice he will perfect in *Pudd'nhead Wilson*. And in his shorter fiction, it is the voice of the two late works that are the most often anthologized: "The Man That Corrupted Hadleyburg" and *The Mysterious Stranger*.

First published in 1899, "The Man That Corrupted Hadleyburg" is about the corruption of a small town and, by extension, America's loss of innocence. We learn, at the onset, that Hadleyburg is "the most honest and upright town in all the region round about it." Because its citizens take pride in its reputation as "an incorruptible town," they make sure that their children have a well-trained moral sense. The town taught "the principles of honest dealing to its babies in the cradle, and made the like teachings the staple of their culture thenceforward through all the years of their education." Unfortunately, the town believes itself to be "sufficient unto itself, and cared not a rap for strangers or their opinions." And in its pride, it subjects a passing stranger to some unnamed offense.

The stranger is "a bitter man and revengeful," and he decides upon a plan to ruin "every man in the place, and every woman—and not in their bodies or in their estate, but in their vanity—the place where feeble and foolish people are most vulnerable." He returns to Hadleyburg at night with a bag that is supposed to contain $40,000 in gold and leaves it with the wife of a poor bank clerk, together with a letter that explains how he owes his success as a gambler to advice given him by one of the townspeople when he was destitute and begging for alms. He claims to have no idea of the man's identity, but he feels confident that the money will find its way to its rightful owner, since the town is famous for its honesty. He says that the man "can be identified by the remark he made to me," and having accomplished his mission, the stranger leaves town, promising never to return.

The reward is advertised in the newspaper. The

Associated Press picks up the story, and by the next morning, "the name of Hadleyburg the Incorruptible was on every lip in America, from Montreal to the Gulf; from the glaciers of Alaska to the orange-groves of Florida; and millions and millions of people were discussing the stranger and his money-sack, and wondering if the right man would be found." But the reader knows that there is no "right man"—the stranger's tale is completely apocryphal. Only one man in Hadleyburg could have been generous to a stranger, Barclay Goodson, and he has been dead for six months, leaving the village "its proper self once more—honest, narrow, self-righteous, and stingy."

In accordance with the instructions in the stranger's letter, a public meeting is called; candidates for the bag of gold are required to present themselves and correctly identify the advice that had made the stranger's fortune. Claims will be verified by matching submissions against the stranger's recollection of the remark, which is kept in a sealed envelope inside the bag and is to be opened at the end of the meeting. Most of the principal citizens of the town quickly convince themselves that they were the unknown benefactor, and they lie awake at night trying to remember what they had never said.

Under the name Howard L. Stephenson, the stranger then sends letters to the nineteen most prominent men in town. Each letter is basically the same, stating that Stephenson had been visiting Barclay Goodson when Goodson gave advice to a beggar that he had later shared with him. Goodson had then gone on to condemn his fellow citizens, but singled out one man in the town for praise, indicating that he owed that man a great debt. Each letter then identifies the recipient as the man Goodson had praised, and "Stephenson" concludes by offering to Goodson's "legitimate heir" the now coveted advice, which he claims to have been: "You are far from being a bad man: Go, and reform." All nineteen fall victim to the temptation of claiming the bag of gold—which proves to be gilded lead—exposing themselves to public exposure as frauds when they each submit an identical message, a mere fragment of the "real" message that is found in the bag: "Go, and reform—or, mark my words—some day, for your sins, you will go to hell or to Hadleyburg—TRY AND MAKE IT THE FORMER." The incorruptible town has been corrupted, its piety no match for its greed.

Through this story, Twain reveals his final view of human nature. The plot is designed to show that men and women are innately corrupt, the most pious among us being capable of deceit if offered the right temptation. His interest in conscience and his scorn for fraud have now come together. What we call "conscience" is simply the ultimate fraud, the result of the way we have been programmed, as opposed to genuine inner strength. This is made clear in an exchange between the bank clerk and his wife, Edward and Mary Richards. Although she is reading the *Missionary Herald* at the beginning of the story and seems to be a good woman, she rebukes her husband for having publicized the money left in their care—he should have hidden it so they could have kept it for themselves. Her husband responds, "But, Mary, you know how we have been trained all our lives long, like the whole village, till it is absolutely second nature to us to stop not a single moment to think when there's an honest thing to be done." Mary recognizes that this is so, but argues that such training is worthless:

"Oh, I know it, I know it—it's been one everlasting training and training and training in honesty—honesty shielded, from the very cradle, against every possible temptation, and so it's *artificial* honesty, and weak as water when temptation comes. . . . God knows I never had shade nor shadow of a doubt of my petrified and indestructible honesty until now—and now, under the very first big and real temptation, I—Edward, it is my belief that this town's honesty is as rotten as mine is; as rotten as yours is."

Almost certainly speaking for Twain, she is proved right by the events that follow. The only notable exceptions to the town's hypocrisy are all outsiders of one sort or another: Rev. Burgess, a minister who has lost his congregation; Barclay Goodson, who had loved a girl with "a spoonful of negro blood in her veins"; and "the loafing, good-natured, no-account" Jack Halliday, a latter-day Muff Potter.

It is clear, however, that the town was never as virtuous as it saw itself. Edward Richards may claim to have always done the honest thing, but long before "the very first big and real temptation" he had helped to ruin Rev. Burgess by keeping to himself evidence that would have proved Burgess innocent of the unspecified crime for which the town wanted to ride him out on a rail. Worried about what others would think, Richards is also a victim, the victim of the town's social structure: "Always at the grind, grind, grind, on a salary—another man's slave, and he sitting at home in his slippers rich and comfortable." And the plutocrats of the town are all mean-spirited. When Jack Halliday sees them smiling, in secret anticipation of securing the bag of gold, he concludes that they must be rejoicing over someone else's misfortune. "He was sure some neighbor of Billson's had broken a leg. . . . The subdued ecstasy in Gregory Yates's face could mean but one thing—he was a mother-in-law short. . . . 'And Pinkerton—Pinkerton—he has collected ten cents that he thought he was going to lose.'"

Even more than St. Petersburg or Dawson's Landing, Hadleyburg is the archetypal American small town. It has a bank and a newspaper, a Presbyterian church and a Baptist church. But, significantly, it is not

on the Mississippi. Twain carefully avoids any details
that would give the town a fixed geography.[4] We are
meant to realize that Hadleyburg could be anywhere.
Similarly, the time is simply "many years ago." We
hear of a camera, a train, and a telegraph office, revealing to us that the action takes place after our industrial fall from primeval grace. But we could be in the
1940s as easily as the 1870s. Independent of particular
time or place, the story has the sort of universality that
is usually associated with fables.

Even more than *Pudd'nhead Wilson*, "The Man
That Corrupted Hadleyburg" is remarkable for its
detachment. It is ironic, but the irony is carefully controlled, as if Twain had finally managed to disassociate
himself from the follies he dissects. James Cox has
described the tone of the story as one of "triumphant
bitterness,"[5] but this is, I think, a mistake. Much of
Twain's later work is very bitter indeed. But, in "The
Man That Corrupted Hadleyburg," Twain moved
beyond bitterness into dispassionate observation,
viewing the culture that had produced him as if from a
great psychic distance. As a result, the story avoids the
stridency that mars so many of the unfinished manuscripts Twain left behind him. It is an indictment, but
an indictment characterized by an air of "high moral
comedy."[6] In the climax of the story, the scene in the
town hall, most of the townspeople have a splendid
time laughing at the discomfiture of the local elite. We
share in that laughter even as we note the gravity of
Twain's charge.

The same cannot be said, however, about *The
Mysterious Stranger*—or "The Chronicle of Young
Satan," as it should be called. The most important of
Twain's shorter works, it is also the most contemptuous.
In various manuscripts, it engaged Twain's attention
from 1897 to 1908 and was "published" only after his
death. His last work, in a manner of speaking, and one
of his most problematic, it must be considered in detail.

Twain had a lifelong fascination with Satan that can be traced to his childhood. In his *Autobiography,* he recorded how his mother was once moved to defend the devil:

She was the natural ally and friend of the friendless. It was believed that, Presbyterian as she was, she could be beguiled into saying a soft word for the devil himself, and so the experiment was tried. The abuse of Satan began; one conspirator after another added his bitter word, his malign reproach, his pitiless censure, till at last, sure enough, the unsuspecting subject of the trick walked into the trap. She admitted that the indictment was sound, that Satan was utterly wicked and abandoned, just as these people had said; *but* would any claim that he had been treated fairly? A sinner was but a sinner; Satan was just that, like the rest. What saves the rest?—their own efforts alone? No—or none might ever be saved. To their feeble efforts is added the mighty help of . . . prayers that go up daily out of all the churches in Christendom and out of myriads upon myriads of pitying hearts. But who prays for Satan? Who . . . has had the common humanity to pray for the sinner that needed it most . . . he being among sinners the supremest?

As an old man, Twain claimed to have tried to write Satan's biography when he was seven. And whether or not this is true, he definitely sounds like his mother's son in "Concerning the Jews," an essay published in *Harper's* the same year as "The Man That Corrupted Hadleyburg":

I have no special regard for Satan; but I can at least claim to have no prejudice against him. It may even be that I lean a little his way, on account of his not having a fair show. All religions issue bibles against him, and say the most injurious things about him, but we never hear his side.

Toward the end of his life, Twain wrote three separate versions of a tale designed to give Satan his say. These works were found among his papers after his death in 1910, and they are usually referred to as the "Eseldorf," "Hannibal," and "Print Shop" manuscripts, collectively known as "The Mysterious Stranger Manuscripts." Twain's own title for the Eseldorf manuscript was "The Chronicle of Young Satan." Heavily edited by Albert Bigelow Paine and Frederick A. Duneka, the general manager of Harper & Brothers, it was published in 1916 under the title *The Mysterious Stranger*. Commonly anthologized, the Paine/Duneka edition remains the version of the work known to most readers.

The story is set in a small town in sixteenth-century Austria, Eseldorf, which can be translated from German as "Assville." The narrator is a man named Theodor Fischer who recounts his experience as a boy when, together with his good friends Nickolaus Bauman and Seppi Wohlmeyer, he met Satan's nephew in the forest outside the town. The boyish-looking nephew is sixteen thousand years old, which is, we are told, quite young for an angel. His name is also "Satan," and he sees nothing embarrassing about this, explaining, "It is a good family—ours," having only one member that has ever sinned. The boys all fall under his spell and watch with fascination as he plays with the lives of the Eseldorf burghers.

As the name of the town suggests, these people are a limited lot—ignorant, foolish, and bigoted. Although nominally ruled by a prince, "neither he nor his family came there oftener than once in five years." It is a world unto itself because "Austria was far away from the world, and asleep, and our village was in the middle of that sleep, being in the middle of Austria." In the absence of temporal power, the Church has much influence. It is represented by two priests, one of whom is rumored to have uttered the heresy that "God was all goodness and would find a way to save all his poor children." This priest, Father Peter, is supplanted by another, Father Adolf, "a very zealous and strenuous priest," held in "solemn and awful respect" because he is so harsh and self-important. But the village is domi-

nated by superstition, and Father Adolf is less important than an astrologer who lives in a tower outside the
town. Although denounced by Father Peter as "a char-
latan—a fraud with no valuable knowledge of any
kind," he is treated with respect by Father Adolf, and
the bishop himself is said to consult with him.

Perceiving Father Peter as a threat, the astrologer
ruins him by repeating to the Bishop his "shocking remark" about God's infinite charity. He is stripped of
his pastoral duties and lives in poverty with his niece
Marget, dependent upon whatever money she can
earn by teaching the harp. Their house is about to be
foreclosed upon when, in order to demonstrate his
power, Satan draws Father Peter into the woods. The
priest loses his wallet, and when he finds it again, it is
filled with eleven hundred ducats—a great fortune.
Father Peter suspects that some enemy has laid a trap
for him, but he uses two hundred ducats to pay his
debts, leaving the rest of the money to collect interest
with a moneylender against the day its true owner
comes to claim it.

As a result of his new wealth, Father Peter is once
again popular in the village, and it looks as if Satan has
done him a good turn. But the astrologer hears about
the money and insists that the priest stole it from him.
Despite the absurdity of his claim, he manages to have
Father Peter imprisoned, and Marget is once again
neglected by the people who had pretended to be her
friends.

Under the name of Philip Traum, Satan visits
Marget and magically provides her with a seemingly
endless supply of luxurious food and drink. No provisions are ever seen to enter the house, however, and
Father Adolf comes to believe that witchcraft is involved. He denounces the house as "bewitched and
accursed," but Satan intervenes to make it seem that
the astrologer is responsible for the larder that super-
naturally replenishes itself. And fulfilling a promise to

the boys, Satan arranges for Father Peter to be found innocent when his case comes to trial, shaping his fate so that he will be happy for the rest of his life. He appears before the prisoner and tells him, "The trial is over, and you stand forever disgraced as a thief." This shock "unseated the old man's reason," and when his friends arrive to tell him that he had been found innocent, they find a madman who believes himself to be the Emperor. Theodor complains that he has been tricked, but Satan argues otherwise:

"Are you so unobservant as not to have found out that sanity and happiness are an impossible combination? No sane man can be happy, for to him life is real and he sees what a fearful thing it is. Only the mad can be happy, and not many of those. . . . I said I would make him permanently happy and I have done it. I have made him happy by the only means possible to his race—and you are not satisfied!"

Reflections of this sort form the real substance of "The Chronicle of Young Satan." The plot is simply a device for helping to bind together a series of Socratic dialogues between Satan and Theodor. Shortly after the resolution of Father Peter's story, the work comes to an abrupt conclusion in which Satan assures his admiring friend that "Life itself is only a vision, a dream" and goes on to offer an almost existential view of life:

"*Nothing* exists; all is a dream. God—man—the world—the sun, the moon, the wilderness of stars—a dream all a dream; they have no existence. *Nothing exists save empty space—and you!*"

He explains his own appearance to Theodor as "but a dream—your dream, creature of your imagination" and promises to "dissolve into nothingness":

"I am perishing already—I am failing—I am passing away. In a little while you will be alone in shoreless space, to wander its limitless solitudes without friend or comrade forever—for you are but a *thought*, the only existent thought, and by your nature inextinguishable, indestructible. . . ."

As metaphysics, Twain's position is sketchy to say the least. But his vision of life as a process of wandering "limitless solitudes," "alone in shoreless space," should be familiar to anyone who has devoted himself to the study of his work as a whole. The pilot in *Life on the Mississippi* suffers "the exquisite misery of uncertainty" because he is lost in "a vague dim sea that is shoreless." Tom Sawyer and Huck Finn often find themselves in a "limitless solitude." And both Hank Morgan and David Wilson are both isolated as well; Hank because he has traveled across time and Wilson because no one in Dawson's Landing is capable of understanding his sense of humor. Different though they are in many respects, Twain's protagonists are all loners, cut off from "friend or comrade forever."

Nonetheless, most readers are disappointed by this conclusion, finding it arbitrary and artificial. It is true that "Traum" means "dream" in German, but nothing else in the story prepares us for a conclusion that tells us everything is a dream. And this is only one of the reservations frequently expressed about the work. Characterization is uncertain. Anachronisms abound. And several scenes sound more suggestive of nineteenth-century Missouri than sixteenth-century Central Europe.

It's hard to believe, for example, that the inn in Eseldorf would have "a nice garden with shade trees reaching down to the riverside, and pleasure boats for hire." This is very civilized for a town where bathing is considered a devilish art, and witches are regularly burned at the stake. The courtroom scene might easily have come straight out of *Tom Sawyer*. And Theodor himself often seems suspiciously similar to Tom. The way he treats Nickolaus—until learning that he is about to die—is very reminiscent of the way Tom had treated his own schoolfellows:

Once at school, when we were eleven, I upset my ink and spoiled four copy-books and was in danger of severe punishment, but I put it on him and he got the whipping.

And only last year I had cheated him in a trade, giving him a large fish-hook which was partly broken through for three small sound ones.

Together with Nickolaus and Seppi, Theodor is easily enchanted by Satan, and we are led, at first, to think that this will be a story of innocence corrupted: "He made us forget everything; we could only listen to him and love him and be his slaves, to do with as he would." Soon after they meet, Satan teaches the boys how to make miniature men and women out of clay, and they laugh at the suffering of the misshapen creatures for whom they are responsible:

Our men and horses were a spectacle to see, they were so little like what they were intended for; for, of course, we had no art in making such things. Satan said they were the worst he had seen, and when he touched them and made them alive, it was just ridiculous the way they acted, on account of their legs not being of uniform length. They reeled and sprawled around as if they were drunk and endangered everybody's lives around them, and finally fell over and lay helpless and kicking. It made us all laugh, though it was shameful to see. The guns were charged with dirt, to fire a salute, but they were so crooked and so badly made that they all burst when they went off, and killed some of the gunners and crippled the others.

Shortly after this, Satan makes a miniature earthquake in which all five hundred of the people die. The boys "could not keep from crying," but Satan cheers them by playing on "a strange, sweet instrument" that "made one mad, for pleasure," and they are soon dancing on the grave of those who died. But after their friendship with Satan has developed further, the boys can still be surprisingly tenderhearted. Theodor gives an apple to an old woman who is about to be executed and he is unable to watch what subsequently transpires, sounding like Huck when he explains, "it was too dreadful, and I went away." And he is very upset when a horrible brute of a man dies without receiving absolution. It could easily be argued that the lingering innocence of the boys serves as a useful foil to Satan's mixture of cynicism and indifference. But we are left wondering how it is that their relationship with Satan does not have a more pronounced effect upon their character.

There are inconsistencies in Satan's character as well. He claims to be disinterested in the affairs of men, but he condemns their folly with passion. He insists that he is immeasurably greater than the boys, and yet he seems strangely eager to impress them with feats of juvenile glory. And as William Gibson has pointed out, he denounces men as "sheep" and "mutton," while speaking to animals in their own language and praising them as morally superior to men.[7]

Twain should not be held altogether responsible for these flaws, however. Had he considered one of the three versions of the story complete, he almost certainly would have published it. He did not, and for this reason alone, it seems hardly fair to complain that the work shows "inventive impulse dissipating into indulgence."[8] Moreover, what appear to be flaws are the result, in many instances, of the way the work was edited. It is important to realize that *The Mysterious Stranger* most readers know is a composite.

In editing *The Mysterious Stranger* for publication, Paine and Duneka took serious liberties with the material. Using "The Chronicle of Young Satan" as their principle text, they lifted the concluding chapter to the Print Shop manuscript, changed the names of the characters in it to "Satan" and "Theodor," announced that they had found the conclusion lying separate in the mass of papers Twain left behind him, and then printed the story without revealing what they had done. So the conclusion that disturbs so many readers disturbs them with good reason—it is not the conclusion for the work to which it is attached. And this is only one of the changes Twain's editors made after his death. Fearing that the work seemed anticlerical, they introduced the character of the astrologer—"borrowing" him from the same manuscript that provided them with both their conclusion and their title—and gave to him the worst of the features originally attributed to Father Adolf.[9] The introduction of the astrologer is probably responsible for their decision to move the story back from 1702, when Twain himself set the action, to 1590. This is a date of their own choosing and a change that requires us to believe that a servant in Eseldorf could have been drinking coffee ninety-three years before the siege of Vienna, when it was introduced to Europe from Turkey. As S. J. Kahn has recently reminded us, "Clemens was an old hand at reporting, and at writing historical fictions, and he was rarely careless about such details. He was merely made to seem careless by Paine's irresponsible editing."[10] And Kahn makes a convincing case in arguing that Paine should have published the Print Shop manuscript as the most coherent of the three versions with which he had to deal.

Incredible though it now seems, Paine and Duneka decided that, as the result of their changes, the text was suitable for children. And after serialization in *Harper's*, it was first published as a children's gift book, with a picture of the astrologer on the cover. One wonders what children could possibly have made of Satan's often quoted definition of man:

Man is made of dirt—I saw him made. . . . Man is a museum of diseases, a home of impurities; he comes today and is gone tomorrow; he begins as dirt and departs as stench.

Representative of the work's tone as a whole, this is not the sort of thing one expects to engage the minds of children as they sit before the yuletide fire. Twain's editors could not have been taking him very seriously.

Satan is altogether contemptuous of mankind; we are, in his view, "so dull and ignorant and trivial and conceited, and so diseased and rickety and such a shabby, poor, worthless lot all around." He proves to Theodor that most men and women are also cowards. In one important scene, a woman is persecuted as a witch because she "was known to have the habit of curing people by devilish arts, such as bathing them . . . and nourishing them instead of bleeding them and purging them . . . in the proper way." Even Theodor joins the mob, explaining that he threw a stone at the woman only because "all were throwing stones and each was watching his neighbor, and if I had not done as the others did it would have been noticed and spoken of." Satan finds this amusing, for he knows that sixty-two of the sixty-eight people throwing stones at the woman had no wish to do so. This becomes a parable for what we like to call civilization, as Satan explains to Theodor:

I know your race. It is made up of sheep. It is governed by minorities, seldom or never by majorities. It suppresses its feelings and its beliefs and follows the handful that make the most noise. . . . The vast majority of the race, whether savage or civilized, are secretly kind-hearted and shrink from inflicting pain, but in the presence of the aggressive minority they don't dare assert themselves. Think of it! One kind-hearted creature spies upon another, and sees to it that he loyally helps in iniquities which revolt both of them.

Foremost among these iniquities is war. Satan takes Theodor and Seppi on a journey through time and space. They watch as Cain kills Abel and are then subjected to a vision of history in which war follows immediately upon war. A "long series of unknown wars, murders, and massacres" is a prelude to the Hebraic wars, in which "the victors massacre the survivors and their cattle."

Next we had the Egyptian wars, Greek wars, Roman wars, hideous drenchings of the earth with blood; and we saw the treacheries of the Romans toward the Carthaginians. . . .

Next Christianity was born. Then ages of Europe passed in review before us, and we saw Christianity and Civilization march hand in hand through those ages, 'leaving Famine and death and desolation in their wake, and other signs of the progress of the human race,' as Satan observed.

Satan then treats the boys to a vision of the future that has proven to be dishearteningly accurate: "He showed us slaughters more terrible in their destruction of life, more devastating in their engines of war, than any we had seen."

If wars have proven to be inevitable, it is because of the cowardice that had prompted Theodor to join in the persecution of a woman who had done no harm. Surveying the history of human warfare, Satan declares:

There has never been a just one, never an honorable one—on the part of the instigator of the war. I can see a million years ahead and this rule will never change in so many as half a dozen instances. The loud little handful—as usual—will shout for war. . . . A few fair men on the other side will argue and reason against the war with speech and pen, and at first will have a hearing and be applauded, but it will not last long; those others will outshout them, and presently the anti-war audiences will thin out and lose popularity. Before long you will see this curious thing: the speakers stoned from the platform, and free speech strangled by hordes of furious men who in their secret hearts are still at one with the stoned speakers—but dare not say so.

But wars are also the result of conscience, or what Satan calls "Moral Sense." It leads man to believe he can distinguish "right" from "wrong" and encourages him to attack the "wrong" with sanctimonious vicious-ness. To illustrate this, Satan takes Theodor to watch a man tortured because he is suspected of heresy:

They asked the man to confess to the charge, and he said he could not, for it was not true. Then they drove splinter after splinter under his nails and he shrieked with the pain. Satan was not disturbed but I could not endure it, and had to be whisked out of there.

Theodor says that torture is "brutal," but Satan disagrees, insisting that it is eminently human:

You should not insult the brutes by such a misuse of that word; they have not deserved it. . . . It is like your paltry race—always lying, always claiming virtues which it hasn't got, always denying them to the higher animals, which alone possess them. No brute ever does a cruel thing—that is the monopoly of those with the Moral Sense. When a brute inflicts pain he does so innocently; it is not wrong; for him there is no such thing as wrong. And he does not inflict pain for the pleasure of inflicting it—only man does that. Inspired by that mongrel Moral Sense of his.

As the scene in the torture chamber suggests, Christians are especially apt to be intolerant, inspired by the dictates of the particular "Moral Sense" they have cultivated. The harshest words in *The Mysterious Stranger* are reserved for the civilization that calls itself Christian. Reflecting upon the progress of the human race, Satan observes:

It is a remarkable progress. In five or six thousand years five or six high civilizations have risen, flourished, commanded the wonder of the world, then faded out and disappeared; and not one of them except the latest ever invented any sweeping and adequate way to kill people. They all did their best—to kill being the chiefest ambition of the human race and the earliest triumph in its history—but only the Christian civilization has scored a triumph to be proud of. Two or three centuries from now it will be recognized that all the competent killers are Christians; then the pagan world will go to school to the Christian—not to acquire his religion, but his guns.

Ironically, Satan's condemnation of the West has proved to be too generous. We have become gun-runners to the world, not in "two or three centuries" but in less than one. But in making this prediction, Twain was giving voice to still another of his concerns—the relationship between the first world and the third, the industrialized West and the colonies it had seized during the ascendancy of imperialism in the nineteenth century.

Toward the end of his life, Twain became increasingly political; his protests against the abuse of colonial power—in works like "King Leopold's Soliloquy" and "To the Person Sitting in Darkness"—are both eloquent and vituperative. And in *The Mysterious Stranger* it is possible to see Twain exploring ideas he would later work out elsewhere. When Satan takes Theodor to China, they see sights "too horrible to think," and the narrator promises "I may go into that by and by and also why Satan chose China for this excursion instead of another place; it would interrupt my tale to do it now." This is almost certainly a reference to the outrages that followed the Boxer Rebellion in 1900, a subject Twain pursued in "To the Person Sitting in Darkness," faithful to his promise to go into it "by and by." And in their final journey together, Satan and Theodor visit India, where Satan takes a cherry seed and makes it grow into a beautiful tree bearing a rich variety of fruit, fruit that the people joyfully begin to gather. But then a foreigner in a white linen suit and sun helmet arrives, exclaiming, "'Away from here! Clear out, you dogs; the tree is on my lands and is my property.'" Satan humbly begs the man to relent, asking him to allow the people "to have their pleasure for an hour," after which he will still have more fruit than he could ever consume. This prompts the colonist to hit Satan with his cane, whereupon "The fruits rotted on the branches, and the leaves withered and fell." Satan then lays the following curse upon the man:

Take good care of the tree, for its health and yours are bound together. It will never bear again, but if you tend it well it will live long. Water its roots once in every hour every night—

and do it yourself; it must not be done by proxy, and to do it in daylight will not answer. If you fail only once in any night, the tree will die, and you likewise. Do not go home to your own country any more—you would not reach there; make no business or pleasure engagements which require you to go outside your gate at night—you cannot afford the risk; do not rent or sell this place—it would be injudicious.

This scene is clearly a parable. Having seized property that is not rightfully his, the colonial planter becomes a slave on his own estate. Because he has dispossessed the people who belong on the land, he can never leave it untended for fear of losing all he has. We see here what George Orwell would later call "the hollowness, the futility of the white man's dominion in the East," his every action determined by the fact that he had to remain in control. Orwell discovered that "when the white man turns tyrant it is his own freedom he destroys,"[11] and this is precisely what Twain had shown more than a generation earlier.

But it should also be recognized that this scene is a parody of the expulsion from Eden. An unrelenting authority figure forbids men to taste the fruit of a tree in his garden, the end result of which is an unalterable sense of loss. And this is only one of several scenes that evoke comparison with Biblical tradition. On his first visit to Marget's house, Satan makes new fish appear in the kitchen, magically replenishing what had already been served, and this naturally calls to mind the miracle of the loaves and fishes. The marriage feast at Cana is suggested by the party at which the wine bottle never empties. And when Satan makes little men and women at the beginning of the story, he is acting like the young Jesus of the *Apocrypha* who made miniature animals out of clay and then gave them life. Apparently suggesting that Satan is divine, Twain is undeniably flirting with heresy, "convinced that whatever shocked his genteel wife would make the foundations of organized Christianity tremble."[12]

It would be a mistake, however, to conclude that
Twain had come to believe in a diabolically controlled
universe. Although Satan has supernatural powers,
he is ultimately helpless, "a puppeteer who cannot
. . . control his puppets."[13] Twain expounds a determinist view of life, in which free will is an illusion and
man's fate entirely predestined. Satan can only play
with the lives of men. He is capable of much mischief,
but he cannot alter the basic order of things—he can
"only laugh in the face of a world he cannot change."[14]
He himself explains the nature of life to Theodor:

Among you boys you have a game: you stand a row of bricks
on end a few inches apart, you push a brick, it knocks its
neighbor over, the neighbor knocks over the next brick—and
so on till all the row is prostrate. That is human life. A child's
first act knocks over the initial brick and the rest will follow
inexorably. If you could see as far into the future as I can,
you would see everything that was going to happen to that
creature, for nothing can change the order of its life after the
first event has determined it. That is, nothing will change it,
because each act unfailingly begets an act, that act begets
another, and so on to the end, and the seer can look forward
down the line and see just when each act is to have birth,
from cradle to grave.

Developing this idea, he argues that even when man

is trying to make up his mind as to whether he will do a thing
or not, that itself is a link, an act, that has its proper place in
his chain; and when he finally decides an act, that also was
the thing which he was absolutely certain to do. You see now
that a man will never drop a link in his chain. He cannot.

As Theodor observes, "He is a prisoner for life."
The result of this system is to reduce men and
women to automata:

Every man is a suffering-machine and a happiness-machine
combined. The two functions work together harmoniously,
with a fine and delicate precision, on the give-and-take principle. For every happiness turned out in the one department

the other stands ready to modify it with a sorrow or a pain—
maybe a dozen. In most cases the man's life is about equally
divided between happiness and unhappiness. When this is
not the case the unhappiness predominates—always, never
the other. Sometimes a man's make and disposition are such
that his misery-machine is able to do nearly all the business.
Such a man goes through life almost ignorant of what happiness is. Everything he touches, everything he does, brings a
misfortune upon him. . . . To that kind of person life is not
an advantage. . . . It is only a disaster.

Given the misfortune that afflicted Twain during
his later years, it is difficult not to believe that he is
drawing here upon the bitterness of his own experience. By the time he began *The Mysterious Stranger,*
he had gone bankrupt and—more importantly—lost
his favorite daughter. What's more, his wife died during the years he sporadically worked on the various
versions of the tale. By reducing life to a mechanistic
formula over which he had no real say, Twain may
have been trying to come to terms with his own miseries. Bernard DeVoto even went so far as to argue that
working on this manuscript helped bring the aged author "back from the edge of insanity," by allowing him
to locate his own troubles at a distance from him:

The miracles, which at first are just an idle game for the
amusement of boys and the astonishment of the villagers,
become finally a spectacle of human life in miniature, with
the suffering diminished to the vanishing point since these
are just puppets, unreal creatures moving in a shadow-play,
and they are seen with the detachment of an immortal spirit,
passionless and untouched. And so from a spectacle they become a dream—the symbolic dream of human experience
that Mark had been trying to write in travail for so many
years.[15]

DeVoto was under the mistaken belief that the Eseldorf manuscript was the last of the three versions of
the story, whereas we now know that it was the first.[16]

We cannot, therefore, subscribe to his belief that it represents Twain's final point of view. Nonetheless, it is reasonable to assume that Twain's personal misfortunes account for much of the harshness in this work, and also for its despair.

Three of the maxims that preface the chapters in *Pudd'nhead Wilson* reveal Twain's conviction that death is a release from sorrow:

Whoever has lived long enough to find out what life is, knows how deep a debt of gratitude we owe to Adam, the first great benefactor of our race. He brought death into the world. (Chapter Three)

Why is it that we rejoice at a birth and grieve at a funeral? It is because we are not the person involved. (Chapter Nine)

All say, "How hard it is to die"—a strange complaint to come from the mouths of people who have had to live. (Chapter Ten)

The Mysterious Stranger goes even further in advocating death over life. As the result of Satan's intervention in Eseldorf, two young children die, but Satan assures Theodor that he is doing them a favor. Nikolaus would otherwise have become "a paralytic log" for forty-six years, "praying for the blessed relief of death." Although he had "a billion possible careers," Satan insists that "not one of them was worth living; they were charged full with miseries and disasters." And Lisa's early death saves her from "ten years of pain," followed by "nineteen years' pollution, shame, depravity, crime, ending with death at the hands of the executioner." Impressed by the visions Satan reveals to him, Theodor reflects, "we do not know good fortune from bad and are always mistaking the one for the other. Many a time since I have heard people pray to God to spare the life of sick persons, but I have never done it."

It is hard to know what to make of this. Twain worked on *The Mysterious Stranger* manuscripts for nearly eleven years, and this suggests that the story was important to him. On the other hand, the fact that he never chose to publish any of the three versions militates against taking their philosophy too seriously. Then again, Twain did leave these manuscripts for others to deal with after his death, while deliberately destroying others.

Our task in evaluating this work is further complicated by the fact that the most cynical observations in it are all spoken by Satan, and we should hesitate before accepting his word as gospel. It is true that he is an unfallen angel—unlike his uncle—but he is still a close relation of what a more religious age than ours called the Arch Fiend. He is a persuasive commentator on human affairs, but cunning is an integral part of the Satanic tradition, and his arguments need not be true simply because they are eloquent. If we were intended to accept these arguments uncritically, why did Twain choose for his mouthpiece a little Satan when there are unfallen angels of less dubious reputation? Moreover, there is a comment in Twain's hand on the back of a notebook he used in 1904 describing as "a foible" Satan's claim that existence is only a dream. As John S. Tuckey has pointed out:

Twain's note may indicate that, unlike his narrator, he did not necessarily accept this solipsistic view as his own; that he perhaps considered the 'life-is-only-a-dream' idea betokened a certain frailty or slight weakness on the part of anyone who would take it altogether seriously.[17]

Twain is often sympathetic to Satan's point of view, but he also sympathizes with the good Father Peter, who defends "Moral Sense" as "the one thing that lifts man above the beasts that perish and makes him heir to immortality!" His sympathies shift back and forth, a common technique in speculative fiction that relies heavily upon irony. Few intelligent readers think Sir

Thomas More admired everything about his Utopians, any more than Jonathan Swift shared Gulliver's adoration of the Houyhnhnms. Twain uses Satan to expose our sins, but he does not identify with him—he leaves that role to his narrator, a lifelong citizen of Assville.

The Mysterious Stranger is thus a work that must be read critically. It is too important to ignore, but too fragmentary to regard as necessarily representative of Twain's final views. While failing to offer a coherent and systematic creed, it offers a clear understanding of the conflicts with which Twain struggled in the last decade of his life, conflicts that can be traced back to the early stages of his work but reach a new degree of intensity within these pages.

When we ask ourselves why Twain was never able to finish *The Mysterious Stranger,* we ask, in effect, what became of him as a writer. His dilemma was familiar: "what to do with little boys about to grow up."[18] But while few of Twain's conclusions are entirely satisfying, the fact remains that he was usually able to finish what he undertook until the 1890s. Fundamentally skeptical, he nevertheless cherished a number of illusions that helped him work out at least a formal resolution. But these illusions gradually slipped away from him.

Despite a strong undercurrent of doubt, *Life on the Mississippi* shows Twain working hard to make himself believe in the reality of "progress." By the end of *A Connecticut Yankee in King Arthur's Court,* he has come to envision the industrial world in an apocalypse of its own making. In *Tom Sawyer* and *Huckleberry Finn,* he looks to the vitality and innocence of children as a source of hope. In *Pudd'nhead Wilson* the juvenile Tom Driscoll is irredeemably wicked, and in *The Mysterious Stranger* the boys are like "the wan ghosts of Huck and Tom,"[19] lacking both imagination and courage. We have seen how Twain was never really able to resolve the conflicts that give meaning to his work. But for most of his career, he was able to pretend that he had done so by keeping alive some alternative to whatever provoked his scorn. The violence of *The Mysterious Stranger* may spring from Twain's inability to imagine any alternative beyond a nihilistic denial of life.

Ultimately one can only speculate as to why Twain never finished *The Mysterious Stranger*. The three manuscripts are all fragmentary, but there are many instances in which Twain allowed inadequately edited material to go into print, if for no other reason than to get it off his desk. On the other hand, if his interest was deeply engaged, Twain could devote years to a work before being willing to part with it. Seven years went into the making of *Huckleberry Finn* and five into *A Connecticut Yankee in King Arthur's Court*. Although the composition of *The Mysterious Stranger* stretched out over eleven years, most of the work familiar to readers was composed in the five years between 1897 and 1902—the year in which Twain signed a contract with Harper & Brothers that guaranteed him a minimum of $25,000 a year. No longer pressed by financial necessity, Twain continued to work sporadically at *The Mysterious Stranger* until 1908. There is no evidence to suggest that Twain was satisfied with what he had done, and it may be that he held back from publication for the simple reason that he no longer needed to worry about money and thus felt himself under no pressure to publish a work with which he was not satisfied.

Twain had always had difficulty with fiction. His earliest works were all variations on the travelogue, and as late as 1882, he was unable to finish *Life on the Mississippi* until he had returned to the river to gather new material to report. He could not return to Eseldorf. And Hannibal itself had changed almost beyond recognition by 1902, when he made his last visit there. Over sixty years old and spiritually exhausted by personal misfortune, Twain experienced a failure of imagination. Prolific until the end of his life, he turned for inspiration to what he read in the newspapers, finding new subjects for his wrath in the Boer War and the Belgian Congo. In a sense, his career can be said to have come full circle—he began as a journalist and ended as a commentator.

Intellectually, Twain was no revolutionary. The contemporary of Nietzsche and Freud, he liked to claim—toward the end of his life—that his ideas were too shocking for publication. But the student of Twain's work as a whole knows otherwise. Remarkable for its vehemence rather than its originality, *The Mysterious Stranger* says nothing that Twain had not said before. It is his angriest work, but the contempt for human nature it embodies is implicit in nearly everything Twain ever wrote.

Confronted with the triumph of folly, Twain held fast to one last belief—his belief in the redemptive power of laughter. Unable to remake the world, he hoped that laughter might check the ignorant armies that clash by night. As Satan explains to Theodor, most men and women

see the comic side of a thousand low-grade and trivial things—broad incongruities, mainly; grotesqueries, absurdities, evokers of the horse-laugh. The ten thousand high-grade comicalities which exist in the world are sealed from their dull vision. Will a day come when the race will detect the funniness of these juvenilities and laugh at them—and by laughing at them destroy them? For your race, in its poverty, has unquestionably one really effective weapon—laughter. Power, money, persuasion, supplication, persecution—these can lift a colossal humbug—push it a little—weaken it a little, century by century, but only laughter can blow it to rags and atoms at a blast. Against the assault of laughter nothing can stand. You are always fussing and fighting with your other weapons. Do you ever use that one? No, you leave it lying rusting. As a race, do you ever use it at all? No, you lack sense and the courage.

This passage accounts for Twain's development from humorist to satirist. Early works, like "The Celebrated Jumping Frog of Calaveras County" and "The Facts Concerning the Recent Carnival of Crime in Connecticut," depend upon "broad incongruities" for their humor; "evokers of the horse-laugh," they are essentially good-humored. But from the mid-eighties on, Twain used laughter as a weapon against "humbug." To laugh at corruption, like the citizens of Hadleyburg, is to "blow it to rags and atoms at a blast." However worthwhile its purpose, such laughter is seldom amusing. It is not the "laughter of affection and self-approval" that converts common failings into a form of pleasure, but a laughter that emphasizes the distance between the wise and the foolish.[20]

It was Twain's misfortune that he came to believe, with Hank Morgan, that all men are fools and that he alone perceived the truth. Increasingly isolated even as he became one of the great celebrities of his age, he became a moralist who saw himself preaching in an empty hall. He began numerous works only to let them drop, and those that he published are characterized by a mocking irony, which could not appease the anger and despair that found relief only in the grave.

Notes

1. THE LINCOLN OF OUR LITERATURE

1. William Dean Howells, *My Mark Twain* (New York: Harper & Brothers, 1910), p. 30.
2. *The Autobiography of Mark Twain*, ed. Charles Neider (New York: Harper & Row, 1959), p. 349. Subsequent quotations attributed to Twain in this chapter are from this work unless otherwise indicated.
3. Annie Adams Fields, as quoted by Justin Kaplan, *Mr. Clemens and Mark Twain* (New York: Simon and Schuster, 1966), p. 149.
4. Albert Bigelow Paine, *Mark Twain* (New York: Harper & Brothers, 1912), pp. 74–75.
5. Bernard DeVoto, *Mark Twain's America* (Cambridge: The Riverside Press, 1932), p. 82.
6. In *The Autobiography*, Twain recalls: "My mother had a good deal of trouble with me but I think she enjoyed it. She had none at all with my brother Henry, who was two years younger than I. . . . I never knew Henry to do a vicious thing toward me or toward anyone else— but he frequently did righteous ones that cost me as heavily. It was his duty to report me, when I needed reporting and neglected to do it myself, and he was very faithful in discharging that duty. He is Sid in Tom Sawyer. But Sid was not Henry. Henry was a much finer and better boy than ever Sid was." Neider, p. 33.
7. Horace Bixby, as quoted by DeLancey Ferguson, *Mark Twain: Man and Legend* (Indianapolis: Bobbs-Merrill, 1943), p. 54.

8. Ferguson, p. 54.

9. *Roughing It*, ed. Franklin R. Rogers and Paul Barender (Berkeley: University of California Press, 1972), p. 43.

10. This name is commonly assumed to have been drawn from his experience on the Mississippi—a myth that Clemens took pains to foster. In *Life on the Mississippi*, he claims to have taken the name from one Captain Isaiah Sellers, who is supposed to have written under that name for the *New Orleans Picayune* in the 1850s: "At the time that the telegraph brought me the news of his death, I was on the Pacific coast. I was a fresh new journalist, and needed a *nom de guerre;* so I confiscated the ancient mariner's discarded one." Scholars have been unable, however, to find reference to "Mark Twain" in either Sellers's journal or any New Orleans newspaper. Moreover, Sellers did not die until March 1864, by which time Clemens had been using "Mark Twain" for over a year. Paul Fatout offers a convincing argument that the name can be traced to Clemens's habit of telling bartenders to "mark twain"—to put, in another words, two more drinks on his tab. Fatout speculates that Twain propagated the Sellers tale because "in pursuit of affluence and respectability in New England, he was well aware that association with a saloon would be damaging in a region less tolerant than the Far West of barroom peccadilloes." See "Mark Twain's Nom de Plume," *American Literature,* 34 (March 1962), pp. 1–7.

11. Susy Clemens, as quoted by Gladys Bellamy, *Mark Twain as a Literary Artist* (Norman, Oklahoma: University of Oklahoma Press, 1950), p. 11.

12. Mary Fairbanks, as quoted by Bellamy, pp. 7–8.

13. Kaplan, p. 44.

14. The man in question, a Dr. Newton, was almost certainly a quack. He charged the Langdons a $1,500 fee for entering Livy's bedroom, raising the shades, and telling her to get out of bed.

15. Kaplan, p. 91.

16. For a firsthand account of life at Quarry Farm, see Clara Clemens, *My Father Mark Twain* (New York: Harper & Brothers, 1931), pp. 59–77.

17. Now the Mark Twain Memorial, it is open to the public.

The house has been carefully restored, and some of
Twain's own furniture is still intact.

18. Kaplan, p. 181.
19. *The Mark Twain-Howells Letters,* ed. Henry Nash
Smith and William M. Gibson (Cambridge: Harvard
University Press, 1960), p. 34.
20. Kaplan, p. 204.
21. *The Autobiography* is laced with sarcastic references to
Harte. Twain claims that the man who came East is not
the man he had known in California: "It was the corpse
of Bret Harte that swept in splendor across the continent . . . and then began a dismal and harassing death-
in-life of borrowing from men and living on women
which was to cease only at the grave." And again: "In
the early days I liked Bret Harte and so did the others,
but by and by I got over it; so did the others. He
couldn't keep a friend permanently. He was bad, distinctly bad; he had no feeling and he had no conscience."
Neider, pp. 127, 294.
22. Howells, p. 60.
23. Kaplan, p. 251.
24. Ibid.
25. Louisa May Alcott, as quoted by Kaplan, p. 268.
26. "Webster was the victim of a cruel neuralgia in the
head. He eased his pain with the new German drug,
phenacetine. The physicians limited his use of it but he
found a way to get it in quantity. . . . He took the drug
with increasing frequency and in increasing quantity. It
stupefied him and he went about as one in a dream. He
ceased from coming to the office except at intervals,
and when he came he was pretty sure to exercise his authority in ways perilous for the business. In his condition, he was not responsible for his acts." Neider, p. 256.
27. *The Mark Twain-Howells Letters,* p. 575.
28. Howells, p. 69.
29. Ibid., p. 101.

2. SAILING A SHORELESS SEA: *Life on the Mississippi*

1. Daniel Ganzel, "Twain, Travel Books, and *Life on the
Mississippi," American Literature,* 34 (March 1962), p. 40.

2. Lafcadio Hearn, review in *New Orleans Times-Demo-crat*, 30 May 1883; reprinted in *Mark Twain: The Critical Heritage*, ed. Frederick Anderson (New York: Barnes & Noble, 1971), pp. 110–11.
3. Leo Marx, *The Machine in the Garden* (New York: Oxford University Press, 1964), p. 321.
4. Roger B. Salomon, *Twain and the Image of History* (New Haven: Yale University Press, 1961), p. 74.
5. Henry Nash Smith, *Mark Twain: The Development of a Writer* (Cambridge: Harvard University Press, 1962), p. 77.
6. This did not happen directly to Twain; it is part of a story he narrates.

3. A HYMN TURNED INTO PROSE: *The Adventures of Tom Sawyer*

1. Robert Regan, *Unpromising Heroes: Mark Twain and His Characters* (Berkeley: The University of California Press, 1966), p. 116.
2. Bernard DeVoto, *Mark Twain's America* (Cambridge: The Riverside Press, 1932), p. 304.
3. Ibid., p. 306.
4. George P. Elliott, "Vacation into Boyhood," afterword to *The Adventures of Tom Sawyer* (New York: New American Library, 1959), p. 221.
5. In the original manuscript, Injun Joe plans to rape the Widow Douglas. Twain was persuaded that this was unsuitable for a book that would be read by children. It seems odd, however, that slitting nostrils and notching ears was considered much more acceptable.
6. Henry Nash Smith makes this point in *Mark Twain: The Development of a Writer* (Cambridge: Harvard University Press, 1962), p. 84.
7. Robert Tracy, "Myth and Reality in *The Adventures of Tom Sawyer*," *The Southern Review*, 4 (Spring 1968), p. 534.
8. Ibid., p. 536.
9. Regan, pp. 116–17.
10. Twain was not the first, however, to rebel against this tradition. B. P. Shillaber, George W. Harris, James M. Bailey, Robert J. Burdette, and Charles B. Lewis all

wrote sympathetically about mischievous boys. And Twain's friend Thomas Bailey Aldrich published *The Story of a Bad Boy* in 1869; its hero shares several characteristics with Tom.

11. Walter Blair, *Mark Twain & Huck Finn* (Berkeley: The University of California Press, 1960), p. 66.

12. In 1907, Twain observed that Theodore Roosevelt was a grown-up Tom Sawyer.

13. For a discussion of Hank Morgan, see chapter 5., pp. 118–28.

14. Smith, p. 89.

15. Both Walter Blair and Robert Regan hold this view.

16. *The Mark Twain-Howells Letters*, ed. Henry Nash Smith and William M. Gibson (Cambridge: Harvard University Press, 1960) p. 91.

17. Twain's contempt for Cooper rivaled his feelings about Scott. He wrote two essays devoted to ridiculing Cooper: "Fenimore Cooper's Literary Offenses" was published in the July 1895 issue of the *North American Review*. "Cooper's Prose Style" remained unpublished until 1946, when it appeared in the September issue of *New England Quarterly;* edited by Bernard DeVoto, it was later included in *Letters from the Earth.* Twain had many objections to Cooper, but his chief complaint was that Cooper's style was unbearably florid.

18. As the text reveals, Twain's intention was confused. Shortly after finishing the book, he wrote, "It is *not* a boy's book, at all. It will only be read by adults. It is only written for adults." (*The Mark Twain-Howells Letters*, p. 91) He later changed his mind, as we know from the Preface. But it is clear that his sense of audience was uncertain.

19. Smith, p. 89.

20. Tracy, p. 540.

21. DeVoto, p. 304.

4.   AN AMERICAN ODYSSEY:
The Adventures of Huckleberry Finn

1. The Concord, Massachusetts, Library Committee, as reported by *The Boston Transcript,* 17 March 1885.

2. Lionel Trilling, introduction to *The Adventures of Huckleberry Finn* (New York: Holt, Rinehart and Winston, 1948), p. vi.

3. For this episode, Twain drew upon Edgar Allan Poe's "Four Beasts in One; or the Royal Homocameleopard" in *Tales of the Grotesque and Arabesque* (1845). See Blair, pp. 319–320.

4. Critics who believe that Tom betrays Jim emphasize the echo here of the forty pieces of silver that Judas received for betraying Christ. The analogy makes little sense, however. It is Jim who receives the money, and Jim is no Judas.

5. Bernard DeVoto, *Mark Twain at Work* (Cambridge: Harvard University Press, 1942), p. 92.

6. Neil Schmitz, "The Paradox of Liberation in *Huckleberry Finn*," *Texas Studies in Literature and Language*, 13 (Spring 1971), p. 135.

7. Leo Marx, "Mr. Eliot, Mr. Trilling, and *Huckleberry Finn*," *American Scholar*, 22 (Autumn 1953), p. 440.

8. Walter Blair, *Mark Twain & Huck Finn* (Berkeley: The University of California Press, 1960), p. 350.

9. Trilling, p. xv.

10. Henry Nash Smith, *Mark Twain: The Development of a Writer* (Cambridge: Harvard University Press, 1962), p. 114.

11. Leo Marx, p. 434.

12. Trilling, p. viii.

13. It is significant, of course, that Twain names a wrecked boat after Walter Scott. A relic of the past, it should be allowed to sink into oblivion—precisely what Twain hoped would happen to Scott's reputation. See chapter two, pp. 43–44.

14. Roger B. Salomon, *Twain and the Image of History* (New Haven: Yale University Press, 1961), p. 165.

15. James Cox, "Remarks on the Sad Initiation of Huckleberry Finn," *Sewanee Review*, 62 (Summer 1954), p. 404.

16. Blair, p. 123.

17. Gladys Bellamy, *Mark Twain as a Literary Artist* (Norman, Oklahoma: University of Oklahoma Press, 1950), pp. 340, 346.

18. David Burg, "Another View of *Huckleberry Finn*,"
     Nineteenth-Century Fiction, 29 (December 1974), p. 318.
19. Smith, p. 124.
20. Ernest Hemingway, *The Green Hills of Africa* (New
     York: Charles Scribner's Sons, 1935), p. 22.

5.   INVINCIBLE STUPIDITY:
A Connecticut Yankee in King Arthur's Court

1. *Mark Twain to Mrs. Fairbanks*, ed. Dixon Wecter (San
    Marino, California: The Huntington Library, 1949),
    p. 257.
2. William Dean Howells, *My Mark Twain* (New York:
    Harper & Brothers, 1910), p. 146.
3. Henry Nash Smith, *Mark Twain's Fable of Progress*
    (New Brunswick, New Jersey: Rutgers University
    Press, 1964), p. 3.
4. Roger B. Salomon, *Twain and the Image of History*
    (New Haven: Yale University Press, 1961), p. 126.
5. Everett Carter, "The Meaning of *A Connecticut Yan-
    kee*," *American Literature*, 50 (November 1978), p. 424.
6. Chadwick Hansen makes this comparison throughout
    "The Once and Future Boss: Mark Twain's Yankee,"
    Nineteenth-Century Fiction, 28 (June 1973), pp. 62–73.
7. Compare the "lonesome" landscapes in which Twain,
    Tom, and Huck all find themselves, pp. 54–55, pp.
    79–80, pp. 108–109.
8. Compare Twain's treatment of the undertaker in *Life
    on the Mississippi*, discussed pp. 37–38.
9. Compare Twain's treatment of conscience in passages
    quoted pp. 83–84, p. 98.
10. Henry Nash Smith, *Mark Twain's Fable of Progress*,
     p. 54.
11. Hansen, p. 70.
12. Ibid., p. 68.
13. Carter, p. 422.
14. Henry Nash Smith, *Mark Twain's Fable of Progress*,
     p. 65.
15. Hansen, p. 71.
16. Judith Fetterley, "Yankee Showman and Reformer:
     The Character of Mark Twain's Hank Morgan," *Texas*

Studies in Literature and Language, 14 (Winter 1973), p. 670.

17.   Salomon, p. 101.
18.   Hansen, p. 70.
19.   Salomon, p. 116.
20.   Carter, p. 423.
21.   James D. Williams, "Revision and Intention in Mark Twain's *A Connecticut Yankee,*" *American Literature,* 36 (November 1964), p. 291.

6.   THE IMITATION WHITE: *Pudd'nhead Wilson*

1.   F. R. Leavis, Introduction to *Pudd'nhead Wilson* (New York: Harcourt, Brace, and World, 1962), p. 9.
2.   Stanley Brodwin, "Blackness and the Adamic Myth in Mark Twain's *Pudd'nhead Wilson,*" *Texas Studies in Literature and Language,* 15 (Spring 1973), p. 167.
3.   James Gargano, "*Pudd'nhead Wilson:* Mark Twain as Genial Satan," *The South Atlantic Quarterly,* 74 (Summer 1975), p. 365.
4.   Malcom Bradbury, Introduction to *Pudd'nhead Wilson* (Harmonsworth, Middlesex: Penguin, 1969), p. 9.
5.   For an examination of the maxims, see William M. Gibson, *The Art of Mark Twain* (New York: Oxford University Press, 1976), pp. 158–176.
6.   Preface to "Those Extraordinary Twins."
7.   The importance of "twins" in the novel is discussed by Marvin Fisher and Michael Elliott, "*Pudd'nhead Wilson:* Half a Dog is Worse than None," *The Southern Review* 8 (Summer 1972), pp. 533–547.
8.   Leavis, p. 21.
9.   Gargano, p. 372.
10.   Henry Nash Smith, *Mark Twain: The Development of a Writer* (Cambridge: Harvard University Press, 1962), p. 176.
11.   Compare Hank Morgan on "training," p. 126.
12.   Brodwin, p. 173.
13.   Twain made a similar point in *A Connecticut Yankee.* Writing about the medieval peasantry, he marveled at

"the alacrity with which this oppressed community had turned their cruel hands against their own class in the interest of the common oppressor." And he drew a parallel with the American South: "It reminded me of a time thirteen centuries away, when the 'poor whites' of our South who were always despised and frequently insulted, by the slave-lords around them, and who owed their base condition simply to the presence of slavery in their midst, were yet pusillanimously ready to side with slave-lords in all political moves for the upholding and perpetuating of slavery, and did also finally shoulder muskets and pour out their lives in an effort to prevent the destruction of that very institution which degraded them."

14. Leslie Fiedler, *Love and Death in the American Novel* (New York: Criterion Books, 1960), p. 389.
15. James Cox, *Mark Twain: The Fate of Humor* (Princeton: Princeton University Press, 1966), p. 236.
16. C. Webster Wheelock, "The Point of Pudd'nhead's Half-a-Dog Joke," *American Notes & Queries*, 8 (June 1970), p. 151.

7. THE GROWTH OF A MISANTHROPE:
Representative Short Fiction

1. Kenneth Lynn, *Mark Twain and Southwestern Humor* (Boston: Little Brown and Co., 1959), p. 204.
2. In "To the Person Sitting in Darkness" (1901), Twain condemns the West for military intervention in China, South Africa, and the Philippines. In "The War Prayer" (1905), a stranger enters a church immediately after the congregation has prayed for God to grant "imperishable honor and glory" to the soldiers of their nation. Announcing that he is a messenger from God, he puts into words the underlying import of the prayer: "O Lord our God, help us to tear their soldiers to bloody shreds with our shells; help us to cover their smiling fields with the pale forms of their patriot dead; help us to drown the thunder of the guns with the shrieks of their

wounded, writhing in pain; help us to lay waste their humble homes with a hurricane of fire; help us to wring the hearts of their unoffending widows with unavailing grief; help us to turn them out roofless with their little children to wander unfriended the wastes of their desolated land in rags and hunger and thirst . . . for our sakes who adore Thee, Lord, blast their hopes, blight their lives, protract their bitter pilgrimage, make heavy their steps, water their way with their tears, stain the white snow with the blood of their wounded feet!"

3. Compare p. 108.
4. Twain does seem to have drawn on memories of one town in particular, however, Fredonia, New York, where his mother lived for several years in the early 1870s. See Leslie F. Chard, "Mark Twain's 'Hadleyburg' and Fredonia, New York," *American Quarterly,* 16 (Winter 1964), pp. 595–601.
5. James Cox, *Mark Twain: The Fate of Humor* (Princeton: Princeton University Press, 1966), p. 265.
6. William M. Gibson, *The Art of Mark Twain* (New York: Oxford University Press, 1976), p. 90.
7. Ibid., p. 198.
8. Cox, p. 272.
9. In the original manuscript, Father Adolf has "fishy eyes" and a "purple fat face"; he also likes to drink, enjoying funerals when "he hadn't too much of a load on, but only enough to make him properly appreciate the sacredness of his office."
10. Sholom J. Kahn, *Mark Twain's Mysterious Stranger: A Study of the Manuscript Texts* (Columbia, Missouri: University of Missouri Press, 1978), p. 24.
11. George Orwell, in "Shooting an Elephant," in *The Orwell Reader,* ed. Richard H. Rovere (New York: Harcourt Brace Jovanovich, 1956), p. 6.
12. Leslie Fiedler, *Love and Death in the American Novel* (New York: Criterion Books, 1960), p. 422.
13. Lynn, p. 284.
14. Ibid.
15. Bernard DeVoto, *Mark Twain at Work* (Cambridge: Harvard University Press, 1942), pp. 127–128.

16. See John S. Tuckey, *Mark Twain and Little Satan* (West Lafayette, Indiana: Purdue University Studies, 1963).
17. Ibid.
18. Cox, p. 282.
19. Lynn, p. 284.
20. Cox, p. 286.

Bibliography

WORKS BY MARK TWAIN

The Celebrated Jumping Frog of Calaveras County, and Other Sketches. New York: Charles Henry Webb, 1867.

The Innocents Abroad. Hartford: American Publishing Company, 1869.

Roughing It. Hartford: American Publishing Company, 1872.

The Gilded Age, with Charles Dudley Warner. Hartford: American Publishing Company, 1873.

"Old Times on the Mississippi." *The Atlantic Monthly* (January–July 1875).

Sketches, New and Old. Hartford: American Publishing Company, 1875.

"The Facts Concerning the Recent Carnival of Crime in Connecticut." *Atlantic Monthly,* (June 1876).

The Adventures of Tom Sawyer. Hartford: American Publishing Company, 1876.

A Tramp Abroad. Hartford: American Publishing Company, 1880.

The Prince and the Pauper. Boston: James R. Osgood & Company, 1881.

Life on the Mississippi. Boston: James R. Osgood & Company, 1883.

The Adventures of Huckleberry Finn. New York: Charles L. Webster & Company, 1884.

"The Private History of a Campaign That Failed." *Century Magazine,* (December 1885).

A Connecticut Yankee in King Arthur's Court. New York: Charles L. Webster & Company, 1889.

The American Claimant (with William Dean Howells). New York: Charles L. Webster & Company, 1892.

Tom Sawyer Abroad. New York: Charles L. Webster & Company, 1894.

The Tragedy of Pudd'nhead Wilson. Hartford: American Publishing Company, 1894.

Personal Recollections of Joan of Arc. New York: Harper & Brothers, 1896.

Tom Sawyer, Detective. New York: Harper & Brothers, 1896.

Following the Equator. Hartford: American Publishing Company, 1897.

"The Man That Corrupted Hadleyburg." *Harper's Magazine,* (December 1899).

"To the Person Sitting in Darkness." *North American Review,* (February 1901).

Adam's Diary. New York: Harper & Brothers, 1904.

King Leopold's Soliloquy. New York: P. R. Warren Company, 1905.

What is Man? Privately printed, 1906.

Christian Science. New York: Harper & Brothers, 1907.

Captain Stormfield's Visit to Heaven. New York: Harper & Brothers, 1907.

Is Shakespeare Dead? New York: Harper & Brothers, 1909.

The Mysterious Stranger. New York: Harper & Brothers, 1916.

The Autobiography of Mark Twain, Charles Neider, ed. New York: Harper & Row, 1959.

Letters from the Earth, Bernard DeVoto, ed., with an introduction by Henry Nash Smith. New York: Harper & Row, 1962.

SELECTED BOOKS AND ARTICLES ON MARK TWAIN

Anderson, Frederick. *Mark Twain: The Critical Heritage.* New York: Barnes and Noble, 1971.

Andrews, Kenneth R. *Nook Farm: Mark Twain's Hartford Circle.* Cambridge: Harvard University Press, 1950.

Baetzhold, Howard. *Mark Twain and John Bull: The British Connection.* Bloomington: Indiana University Press, 1970.

Bellamy, Gladys. *Mark Twain as a Literary Artist.* Norman, Oklahoma: University of Oklahoma Press, 1950.

Blair, Walter. *Mark Twain & Huck Finn.* Berkeley: University of California Press, 1960.

Branch, Edgar Marquess. *The Literary Apprenticeship of Mark Twain.* Urbana: University of Illinois Press, 1950.

Briden, Earl F. "Idiots First, Then Juries: Legal Metaphors in Mark Twain's *Pudd'nhead Wilson.*" *Texas Studies in Literature and Language,* 20 (Spring 1978), 169-180.

Brodwin, Stanley. "Blackness and the Adamic Myth in Mark Twain's *Pudd'nhead Wilson.*" *Texas Studies in Literature and Language,* 15 (Spring 1973), 167-176.

Brooks, Van Wyck. *The Ordeal of Mark Twain.* New York: E. P. Dutton & Company, 1920.

Budd, Louis J. *Mark Twain: Social Philosopher.* Bloomington: Indiana University Press, 1962.

Burde, Edgar J. "Mark Twain: The Writer as Pilot." *PMLA,* 93 (October 1978), 878-892.

Burg, David. "Another View of *Huckleberry Finn.*" *Nineteenth Century Fiction,* 29 (December 1974), 299-319.

Canby, Henry Seidel. *Turn West, Turn East: Mark Twain and Henry James.* Cambridge: The Riverside Press, 1951.

Carkeet, David. "The Dialects in *Huckleberry Finn.*" *American Literature,* 51 (November 1979), 315-332.

Carter, Everett. "The Meaning of *A Connecticut Yankee.*" *American Literature,* 50 (November 1978), 418-440.

Chard, Leslie. "Mark Twain's 'Hadleyburg' and Fredonia, New York." *American Quarterly,* 16 (Winter 1964), 595-601.

Cox, James. "Remarks on the Sad Initiation of Huckleberry Finn." *Sewanee Review,* 62 (Summer 1954), 389-405.

————. *Mark Twain: The Fate of Humor.* Princeton: Princeton University Press, 1966.

DeVoto, Bernard. *Mark Twain's America.* Cambridge: The Riverside Press, 1932.

————. *Mark Twain at Work.* Cambridge: Harvard University Press, 1942.

Fatout, Paul. "Mark Twain's Nom de Plume." *American Literature*, 34 (March 1962), 1–7.

Ferguson, DeLancey. *Mark Twain: Man and Legend*. Indianapolis: Bobbs-Merrill, 1943.

Fetterley, Judith. "Yankee Showman and Reformer: The Character of Mark Twain's Hank Morgan." *Texas Studies in Literature and Language*, 14 (Winter 1973), 667–679.

Fisher, Marvin, and Michael Elliott. "*Pudd'nhead Wilson:* Half a Dog is Worse than None." *Southern Review*, 8 (Summer 1972), 533–547.

Ganzel, Daniel. "Twain, Travel Books, and *Life on the Mississippi.*" *American Literature*, 34 (March 1962), 40–55.

Gargano, James. "*Pudd'nhead Wilson:* Mark Twain as Genial Satan." *South Atlantic Quarterly*, 74 (Summer 1975), 365–375.

Gibson, William M. *The Art of Mark Twain*. New York: Oxford University Press, 1976.

Girgus, Sam B. "Conscience in Connecticut: Civilization and its Discontents in Twain's Camelot." *New England Quarterly*, 51 (December 1978), 547–560.

Gribben, Alan. "The Master Hand of Old Malory: Mark Twain's Acquaintance with *Le Morte d'Arthur.*" *English Language Notes*, 16 (September 1978), 32–40.

Hansen, Chadwick. "The Once and Future Boss: Mark Twain's Yankee." *Nineteenth Century Fiction*, 28 (June 1973), 62–73.

Howells, William Dean. *My Mark Twain*. New York: Harper & Brothers, 1910.

Kahn, Sholom J. *Mark Twain's Mysterious Stranger: A Study of the Manuscript Texts*. Columbia, Missouri: University of Missouri Press, 1978.

Kaplan, Justin. *Mr. Clemens and Mark Twain*. New York: Simon and Schuster, 1966.

Ketterer, David. "Epoch-Eclipse and Apocalypse: Special 'Effects' in *A Connecticut Yankee. PMLA*, 88 (October 1973), 1104–1113.

King, Bruce. "*Huckleberry Finn.*" *Ariel*, 2 (October 1971), 69–77.

Lynn, Kenneth S. *Mark Twain and Southwestern Humor*. Boston: Little, Brown & Company, 1959.

————. "Welcome Back from the Raft, Huck Honey!" *American Scholar*, 46 (Summer 1977), 338–347.

Marx, Leo. "Mr. Eliot, Mr. Trilling, and *Huckleberry Finn*." *American Scholar*, 22 (Autumn 1953), 423–440.

Masters, Edgar Lee. *Mark Twain: A Portrait*. New York: Charles Scribner's Sons, 1938.

Paine, Albert Bigelow. *Mark Twain: A Biography*. New York: Harper & Brothers, 1912.

Regan, Robert. *Unpromising Heroes: Mark Twain and His Characters*. Berkeley: University of California Press, 1966.

Rogers, Franklin R. *Mark Twain's Burlesque Patterns*. Dallas: Southern Methodist University Press, 1960.

Rogers, Rodney O. "Twain, Taine, and Lecky: The Genesis of a Passage in *A Connecticut Yankee*." *Modern Language Quarterly*, 34 (December 1973), 436–447.

Salomon, Roger B. *Twain and the Image of History*. New Haven: Yale University Press, 1961.

Schmitz, Neil. "The Paradox of Liberation in *Huckleberry Finn*." *Texas Studies in Literature and Language*, 13 (Spring 1971), 125–136.

Smith, Henry Nash. *Mark Twain: The Development of a Writer*. Cambridge: Harvard University Press, 1962.

————. *Mark Twain's Fable of Progress*. New Brunswick, New Jersey: Rutgers University Press, 1964.

Spangler, George M. "*Pudd'nhead Wilson:* A Parable of Property." *American Literature*, 42 (March 1970), 28–37.

Tracy, Robert. "Myth and Reality in *The Adventures of Tom Sawyer*." *Southern Review*, 4 (Spring 1968), 530–541.

Tuckey, John S. *Mark Twain and Little Satan*. West Lafayette, Indiana: Purdue University Studies, 1963.

Warren, Robert Penn. "Mark Twain." *Southern Review*, 8 (Summer 1972), 459–492.

Wheelock, C. Webster. "The Point of Pudd'nhead's Half-a-Dog Joke." *American Notes & Queries*, 8 (June 1970), 150–151.

Williams, James D. "Revision and Intention in Mark Twain's *A Connecticut Yankee*." *American Literature*, 36 (November 1964), 288–297.

————. "The Use of History in Mark Twain's *A Connecticut Yankee*." *PMLA*, 80 (March 1965), 102–110.

Index

Selected list of titles (continued from page ii)

MARIANNE MOORE   *Elizabeth Phillips*
VLADIMIR NABOKOV   *Donald E. Morton*
THE NOVELS OF HENRY JAMES   *Edward Wagenknecht*
JOYCE CAROL OATES   *Ellen G. Friedman*
FLANNERY O'CONNOR   *Dorothy Tuck McFarland*
GEORGE ORWELL   *Roberta Kalechofsky*
KATHERINE ANNE PORTER   *John Edward Hardy*
EZRA POUND   *Jeannette Lander*
MORDECAI RICHLER   *Arnold E. Davidson*
PHILIP ROTH   *Judith Jones and Guinevera Nance*
J. D. SALINGER   *James Lundquist*
UPTON SINCLAIR   *Jon Yoder*
ISAAC BASHEVIS SINGER   *Irving Malin*
CHRISTINA STEAD   *Joan Lidoff*
LINCOLN STEFFENS   *Robert Stinson*
JOHN STEINBECK   *Paul McCarthy*
J. R. R. TOLKIEN   *Katharyn F. Crabbe*
LIONEL TRILLING   *Edward Joseph Shoben, Jr.*
JOHN UPDIKE   *Suzanne Henning Uphaus*
GORE VIDAL   *Robert F. Kiernan*
KURT VONNEGUT   *James Lundquist*
ROBERT PENN WARREN   *Katherine Snipes*
EUDORA WELTY   *Elizabeth Evans*
EDITH WHARTON   *Richard H. Lawson*
OSCAR WILDE   *Robert Keith Miller*
THORNTON WILDER   *Hermann Stresau*
VIRGINIA WOOLF   *Manly Johnson*
RICHARD WRIGHT   *David Bakish*

Complete list of titles in the series available from publisher on request.